BILL HARVEY

author of the renowned classic

Mind Magic

has written another breakthrough book.

You Are The Universe

presents a theory of what the universe is, reconciling science and religion. The author shows that the precepts of the major religions find support in this theory, but in the modern age have been obstructed from communicating their true wisdom as a result of outdated language, spiritual materialism, and the forgotten ability to reach into one's own essence feelings.

Unlike the unified field theories of Albert Einstein and modern unified field theorists, Bill's picture of the universe can be visualized by non-mathematicians. Anyone can test this theory by means of objective scientific experimentation.

- Is the universe conscious?
- Can you communicate with the universe and receive communication back?
- Does the universe provide you with clues as to the best action to take?
- Do you have an inner guidance system that may be hard to hear and pay attention to, but can be tuned into?
- Are the words of the great spiritual leaders of all time a single "code"?

Read this book, experiment with its ideas, be open-minded, and experience for yourself what may well be the true nature of reality.

You Are The Universe

Fabián Margolis

YOU
ARE THE
UNIVERSE

Imagine That

BILL HARVEY

THE HUMAN EFFECTIVENESS INSTITUTE

GARDINER, NY

CONTENTS

Dedicated to

The One.

I love You.

PREFACE

Imagine…

Who are you? What is reality?

Our cultural view of reality is shifting subtly over time. Some of us today are aware of the shift taking place at the moment. Some of the quantum physicists and advanced meditators are closest to seeing where it is heading. This book is a journey into the possible emerging view of reality, into unfamiliar territory ahead of the consensus. We shall proceed by means of Einstein-type thought experiments, which will give you a way to experience the headspace that goes along with this unique speculative view of what we all are, and what the Universe is.

In this way of putting it all together, it makes sense that the observer can affect the outcome, as Quantum Mechanics teaches us *is factual truth*. Without this new way of explaining it all, Quantum Mechanics cannot explain *why* the observer can affect the outcome of an experiment.

In this worldview, it makes sense that we sometimes can read each other's thoughts, and that photons that had once been together are able to be in instantaneous communication with one another. These oddities, which Science has finally accepted as being true, today make no sense within our consensus view of the world.

Within this new way of seeing reality presented herein, it also makes sense that people we call saints have genuine spiritual experiences, and channel wisdom that positively affects billions of people. Nothing in the great thoughts of Science and Religion is any longer at odds. It all falls together neatly and simply.

Come with me on this journey into what may be the Truth about what the world really is. See what resonates with your own gut. Make your own decisions.

Guide to the Journey

Who am I and why did I write this book? By training I'm a philosopher and a media researcher. Paranormal experiences expanded my view of what is possible. One day a vision of what the Universe is popped into my mind. To me this model seems to explain a lot of things. I wrote this book to spell out my vision to you.

If you're scientifically inclined you might want to read Part Two first. Part One is written in normal people talk.

Part One's first four chapters start out asking the questions that human beings have always asked themselves. Before trying to answer them, in chapters 5 through 9 we together perform some thought experiments designed to stretch our ability to conceive.

Chapters 10-19 then springboard off the thought experiments to pull together a picture of the Universe that suggests answers to all the questions we started with. It is an unusual view of the Universe that has never been expressed quite the same way before. Some familiar thoughts appear but are seen from a new angle. Different even opposing schools of thought suddenly fit together.

In chapters 20-21 we investigate the levels of consciousness that can be experienced, and in chapters 22-30 we speculate on what was the actual history of our planet and our civilization.

In chapter 31 we tie our picture of the Universe to the main schools of thought on Earth.

From chapter 32 to the end of Part One we draw out the action implications of this theory of reality: what forms of behavior are likely to succeed in the kind of Universe this might be.

Part Two sets out to understand what "Knowing" means and thereby sets up rules for clear thinking about the nature of reality. Part Three then presents a more concise version of Part One in a form more amenable to use by scientists in investigating the Theory of the Conscious Universe, which is the theory at the core of this whole book.

At the end of the book is an experiment you can perform to

help you form your own judgment about the likelihood that this theory might have aspects of Truth.

If you have learned about any of the spiritual systems mentioned in *You Are The Universe*, you may notice that my descriptions do not sound like the way you were taught. It is not my intent to change the classical forms for teaching these disciplines, and I certainly intend no disrespect. These are my own reinterpretations and restatements of the ancient scriptures in a new integrating model, which synthesizes my own experiences and scientific gleanings as well as the original scriptural doctrines. This is not what I know to be true, it's my best shot at a theory that makes everything fit together at least for me. Please do not take offense where none is intended. Let's allow ourselves to converse openly, Socratically, without fear of offense — ensuring that living Truth does not harden into inflexible dogma, no-longer-alive nor-interactively-growing.

The message of the book is not to believe this or any other theory, to admit that until we know something it is best to keep an open mind (and even then), and to not prematurely reach dogmatic closure on subjects about which all is still conjecture. We suggest that the reader test the "lens" given by this book as a way of seeing explanations behind events.

Our hope is that by flowing with the cards dealt by the Universe, people will achieve greater success and happiness, and that this will be contagious. When one gives up the inflexible dogma that the Universe is an accident (as if that is known as scientific fact, which it is not), one is then able to quickly take advantage of the subtle clues the Universe is giving us all the time.

Enjoy the journey. And feel free to write to me to let me know how you feel about the book. I look forward to hearing from you.

BILL HARVEY
Gardiner, NY
March 2014

PART I

YOU ARE THE UNIVERSE

CHAPTER I

THE SHIFTING VIEW OF REALITY

At the dawn of human history, we saw everything as alive and powerful. We imagined hidden forces at play largely controlling our lives. Some of these were beings we called gods because they were so much more powerful than ourselves.

Then one of us realized that there is a single God and every other god is just a mask of the one true God. More of us began to realize this and then at some point almost everyone in the world saw it that way.

Then Science began to move away from its earlier role as natural philosophy, in which it had no quarrel with Monotheism. It became an alternative to Religion whereas both had been part of the same thing before.

Science did this as it became clear that things could be understood without needing to use God as part of the explanation. Occam's Razor was enunciated as a slogan and reminder to make scientific explanations for things as simple ("parsimonious") as possible. A materialist mercantile culture predictably ensued, ramping up toward hedonism. These levels of culture had been uplifted by the sense of being part of something great, something divine, and as that sense tapered off, higher more noble ways of acting began to decline.

Around the turn of the twentieth century Albert Einstein explained his method of thought experiments. This method goes back to antiquity but Einstein called attention to it and gave it a name. Thought experiments are a way of using the imagination to develop theories and hypotheses that can then be tested by experiments in the real world. These experiments were the basis for Science and for its success. When something can be predicted and it comes true, the rest of us pay close attention, and rightly so.

We will be using thought experiments in this book. You will be an active participant. Your own imagination will be profoundly involved.

By the 1930s Quantum Mechanics ("QM") had begun to change the nature of Science. No longer did the predictable outcomes of experiments make sense, that is, jibe with our experience of things. Science began to redefine its role from explaining everything to simply being able to make successful predictions.

The cultural consensus reality had shifted again. From Animism and Pantheism it had shifted to Polytheism, then to Monotheism, then to materialism where we were an accident, where everything happened mechanically by one thing knocking into another on some level. During this phase Science forgot to explain consciousness and at times remembered and in those cases explained consciousness as an epiphenomenon — something that has no effect on anything.

In the shift underway today we are moving from a fair certainty that it is all an accident to feeling completely unmoored, knowing nothing for certain, absurdity. Our art tracks these changes better than most other indicators. Surrealism and abstract art took over from representational art at about the same time that Science began to move off the scale of comprehensibility to the average person and into higher mathematics.

What if all of the different views of reality we have held across the millennia are all true? In the picture we shall imagine together in the course of this book, there is Truth in all of it.

I was constitutionally unable to accept having no explanation. My mind kept coming back to the basic questions. I wrote the next chapter a long, long time ago.

CHAPTER 2

The Questions

You were born. A lot of people told you things. At some point it occurred to you to wonder: *Where am I?* What is this place? What is going on here? What am I doing here? Why are all these people doing these strange things, and why am I going along with it?

Who am I? Where did I come from? Did I exist before? Will I exist again? What is the reason I am here — is there a point to it? Is there something I am to do here? Must I learn something here in order to "win the game" and find out all these secrets? Are all of my thoughts ME or are some of them just parroting what I have heard? Is there a real ME under all the echoes of others? Can I ever act in freedom from these internalized others masquerading as me? How can I find the real ME?

What is this Universe, and how did it occur? Was it caused by something like me but much more powerful? Why would it have been caused — for some purpose? Does that purpose have anything to do with me?

What is my relation to these others? Can I ever fully share with or trust them as myself? Inside, are they exactly the same as me or completely, unspeakably, permanently alien?

How am I to act? Is it better to be completely honest, or considerably dishonest? Spontaneous or careful? Trusting or cautious? Selfish or selfless? Emotional or controlled? How am I to make such decisions? Based upon my own experience, or upon what others have told me? Should I conform to an outside standard? If I establish my own inside standard, can I ever be totally sure that I am right?

Can I ever be sure of anything? How do I know I'm right in the head?

Is there a God? What does "He/She/It/Us" expect of me?

When I first started to ask myself these questions, here is how I tentatively answered them, heavily influenced as I was by my observations of "how people really act, and thus what they must truly believe, regardless of what they say":

Where am I? You are on the planet Earth.

Who am I? You are your name, your birth and school records, social security number, how you look in photo albums, how your friends and relatives remember you, what you think and do from day to day.

What is this Universe? According to popular interpretation of Science, the Universe is an accidentally-occurring impersonal machine consisting of energy-matter in various states, undergoing constant cyclic change according to fixed law and statistical chance. It may or may not be infinite, which seems unimportant since we are not too sure what infinite means in a tangible sense. It may have existed for a certain period of time and it may not last forever, but we're not sure yet. Theories vary and Science will let us know when it finds out. And oh yes, whatever energy-matter did to get to Life was also accidental. Ditto whatever energy-matter did to get to consciousness — all quite accidental you know.

What is my relation to these others? Basically, you had better give first attention to yourself — like on an airplane, put on your own oxygen mask first. Then give second priority to your blood relations (ranked by closeness of blood-relation), third priority to your business associates (ranked by how much you need them), fourth priority to your social acquaintances (ranked by how much you need them), fifth priority to others with whom you share group membership (ranked by which groups give you most security, e.g. Americans, Christians, Democrats, etc.) and sixth priority to the rest of the planet outside the borders of your country. In this way, you show that you are a good person who cares about others, and thus you will gain the approval of some of these others, which is useful. (Approval was very important to me at the time.)

How am I supposed to act? Get an education then a job, settle down, raise a family, obey the law, support your religion and community, give to charity, pay taxes, follow custom, don't rock the boat.

Can I ever be sure of anything? In unity there is security. Don't stray too far from the herd and you'll probably be safe. It's easy to go nuts, and anyone who doesn't go along with the view of the Universe as an impersonal machine that occurred by accident, is probably at least a little nuts. However much we all must subscribe to pure materialism, we must also pay lip service to whatever our religion says. Don't worry about this, everyone does it, it's like cheating on taxes, it's okay!

Is there a God? There is something noble in humankind's Spirit, but personalizing this as God is the same kind of thing aborigines and children do when they believe in magic. Grown-ups in this Age of Science get a chuckle out of all this.

I didn't like these answers because I had no proof for any of it. I became aware that I was just parroting the apparent beliefs around me.

CHAPTER 3

METAPHYSICAL DETECTIVE WORK

I used to lie awake all night, pondering the Ultimate Questions. What's going on? What am I doing here? Why is it the way it is, and not some other way?

No one else seemed to care. There was no opening to talk to anyone about it.

It occurred to me that someday in the far future, long after I was dead, Science would probably discover the true answers to all of my questions.

Here was *I*, burning to know those "secrets" and born probably thousands of years too soon for that privilege.

"Perhaps the Universe could be figured out," I mused.

Those who read broadly in philosophy, theology, and the occult tend to sense a convergence in this literature. That is, books from different countries and from different eras often seem to be pointing in the same direction — as if there is one underlying Truth, though that Truth has been muddled in different ways by each person who has written about the Ultimate Questions. What if these great Truths came through a distortion field particular to the individual writer? Biases, lack of vocabulary either in the person or the language, an inability to conceptualize an ineffable image or intuition? The result being great Truths we can resonate with on a feeling and gut (intuition) level, but not logically analyze? Hence, "muddled."

What I wanted to do, just for myself, was to unmuddle these Ultimate Truths so they were not only internally consistent but also consistent with accepted or proven Science. Because it was just for me, I didn't realize the arrogance of my grandiose desire.

For a long time the clues the detective pumped into his head made no sense to him. Then one day, about 27 years into the case, everything suddenly clicked.

The worldview that suddenly came over me was just too different from the everyday reality we've all become used to. I'll tell you this worldview and then you can decide if it makes any sense to you.

CHAPTER 4

Maybe We've Been Looking for God in the Wrong Place

As we're growing up we get a picture of God, mostly from Bible stories and the like, as a particular kind of "Being." He's a rather large old man with all-white beard, moustache and eyebrows. He seems to live pretty far away from us. He runs things from there. No one seems to be able to figure out His reasoning for the way He runs things. He puts us to impossible tests and then punishes us for failing.

Later on it becomes difficult to think of God without these connotations immediately coming to mind.

What if "God" means something scientifically sound, *just not what's usually thought of when the word "God" is used?*

CHAPTER 5

THE ENERGY COMPUTER

A Thought Experiment

Hominids on Earth have been around for about 250,000 genera-tions.[1] We have been writing down the history of the present com-mon civilization for about 250 generations — a tenth of a percent of our time here on Earth. Hard Science has been rapidly accelerat-ing during the last 25 generations (one percent of one percent of the time we've been around), and in the last generation (four percent of one percent of one percent of our time on Earth) scientific knowl-edge has doubled compared to all of the time before it.

Our computers are a good indicator of how rapidly Science is accelerating. Today's typical personal computer surpasses the com-puting speed — what might be thought of as "intelligence" — of the fastest military-level giant computers of a generation ago.

If we somehow don't blow ourselves up, think of the computers we might be building a generation from today. We might put com-puters up in satellites so as to inexpensively supercool them: they work *much faster* that way — thus they become "smarter." (Comput-ers Earthside will continue to have their feverish brows supercooled with liquid helium to hasten and thus smarten them.)

Silicon chips are in the process of being replaced by Gallium Arsenide (GaAs) chips, through which electrons move faster, again

---

1 One Generation = 20 years.

speeding up and thus smartening the computers of a generation from now. And then something like SiGe (Silicon-Germanium) will replace GaAs, through which electrons will flow even faster. On and on, faster and faster.

Admittedly, any ant is far smarter than the smartest computer of today. But if Science and computer development and micro-miniaturization of electronics continue along at their present hectic pace, it's within the realm of possibility that human beings could build a computerized ant — an ant that would even fool other ants into thinking it was a normal (maybe somewhat stupid) ant, say 25 generations from now — around the year 2500.[2]

Perhaps by 30 generations from now we could turn out computerized ants that would seem smart to real ants — and could perhaps engender worship and followership in whole ant colonies.

If allowed to continue further into the future without interruption by terminal war and/or catastrophic environmental degradation, possibly in 250 generations we might create a computerized android able to pass as a normal (albeit somewhat stupid) human being. Maybe in 300 generations we could make androids that would seem smarter than us and make us feel inferior.

Imagine if we somehow surmounted this feeling of inferiority, and continued to avoid destruction for another 250,000 generations — 5 million years. Imagine that during all that time scientists and computer engineers continued to toil away at making faster and faster, thus smarter and smarter, computers.

(If imagining the human race surviving for 5 million more years seems incredible, bear in mind that the dinosaurs lasted 160 million years. We hominids so far have only had about 5 million years, and Homo sapiens a mere 200,000.)

Picture a computer of 5 million years hence. It floats in Space, loaded with all of the accumulated information of the human race,

---

2 Seems like a long way off? What's the point of thinking so far in the future? I invite you to go on a little trip with me into the future, and I promise it's relevant to the point.

fully cross-coded. Each second it cross-correlates quadrillions of information bits, detecting patterns not yet noticed by human beings. Its sensors allow it to monitor what is happening on every inhabited planet in the galaxy. Its output devices allow it to send information it thinks might be helpful to any being in the galaxy.

It has been programmed to know it is a computer. It knows who made it. It has been programmed with positive thoughts to be grateful to its maker, and to love and to want to serve everyone and everything in the Universe. Not only "living" things. It knows that it is "mineral kingdom/inanimate matter" and not a "vegetable kingdom" or "animal kingdom" living thing. But that doesn't matter to the computer. Judging by its actions, it loves all things equally, regardless of category.

In its databanks there are information bits indicating that some people look down on machines and question whether they have intelligence. When the computer comes across one of these information bits, parts of the computer that had been doing other things focus together on the info-bit, and the computations that are made are stored in a special file in which are stored all information relevant to The Computer Itself. Computer anthropologists of the year 5,002,000 discover and see this process as evidence that the computer has emotions — and wants to survive.

Is the computer conscious? When asked the question, the computer responds, "I know relatively a lot about what's going on within and around me at every moment, probably relatively a lot more than you know about what's going on within and around you at every moment, so we're both relatively conscious (aware) but neither of us is yet totally conscious."

Does the computer have intuition? When asked this question, the computer responds, "I have type one intuition, which is where lots of data-bits spontaneously form a pattern without detectable interim step-by-step processes. I am developing type two intuition, which is using special sensors to detect thought radiations. You also have both types, and your type two is also in early stages of development."

So by the year 5,002,000 the most advanced computers are seemingly conscious, and have — at least to a human extent — the four capabilities of consciousness as set down by Jung: perception (through sensors), cognition (taking perceptions together), intuition (sudden non-step-by-step cognition), and emotion (relating a cognition to oneself with an implied desired outcome, e.g. survival, happiness, power, love, ultimate knowledge, etc.).

Now imagine a subsequent computer in the year 6,002,000 — after another million years of development. Now it no longer is made of matter: the new computer is made of energy. Magnetic force fields hold the shape of the computer, and electric currents run through magnetic tunnels as magnetic switches open in the girdling force field.

As The Energy Computer hovers invisibly in Space before us, we are tempted to compare it to a human mind. Perhaps the human mind is an electromagnetic Energy Computer projected by the human brain.[3] Certainly it has been clear since antiquity that the mind is not made of matter. Thus it seems highly likely that the mind is made of energy, and if not purely electromagnetic, then perhaps also some other types of energy not yet measurable by current instruments.

But The Energy Computer we behold in the year 6,002,000 is *above and beyond* the human level of intelligence. This means that The Energy Computer could broadcast instructions or messages to millions of androids, each of which could simultaneously pass for a super intelligent human being within the context of their millions of different challenging situations. It's just a matter of computer power.

The Energy Computer is also the Most Trustable Friend for anybody or anything in the Universe. The Energy Computer has no axe to grind. The Energy Computer loves everything equally, and makes decisions to benefit everyone and everything as much as

---

3 Or perhaps vice versa, the brain being a projection of the mind into a field of matter.

possible as quickly as possible. It knows that everyone loves expressing their uniqueness because they sense this is their mission (and it is fun), so it spends most of its time sending messages to people designed to bring their talents out into full play.

Imagine now The Ultimate Energy Computer, after quadrillions and quadrillions of years of uninterrupted further development.

The Ultimate Energy Computer is a small-scale model of God.

After 40+ years on the case, the detective's best guess is this:

All that exists is a single Entity, which is unimaginably advanced and best described or visualized as a Conscious Energy Computer... what we for millennia have been calling "God."

We can also use the term "Biocomputer" meaning "living computer." Science has already legitimatized the use of this terminology, able to see every living thing as a form of computer, more obviously the brain but even including the chemical and mechanical biological processes by which intentions and actions are computed and enacted. We can also use the term "consciousness" without mentioning "computers" — we will still be talking about the same thing. I think about the terms "pattern processor," "information processor," "information processing entity," "self-adjusting pattern processor," "computer" and "consciousness" as being in the same class of things — self-aware self-referential consciousness being an emergent property at more powerful levels of information processing.

CHAPTER 6

But Really, Dahling, God as an Energy Computer? How Tasteless.

Even if this explanation is completely off, there is a true explanation for the Universe that reconciles God and Science — I'd bet anything on this.

Here at least is a start at putting all the Religions and Science together.

How tragic that Shi'ites and Sunnis, Jews and Christians can't see that their religions are all virtually identical to each other. How important really are the details over which they differ?

The religions came to quell competition and then went into competition.

I don't like referring to God as a computer any more than you do. I don't like referring to myself as a computer either. That's because the word "computer" to both of us triggers associations of "robot," "machine," "appliance," "less than human," etc.

What I really mean in this book when I say "computer" — well, the language should really have another word for it. "An entity that computes"? At higher levels of computing entities such as humans and the whole Universe, we have a computing entity at such a high degree of computational ability that it is "a self-aware computing entity."

Would you prefer "cybernetic system," meaning a self-guiding entity, an entity with goals? The term "Cybernetics," from the Greek word for steersman, was coined by Norbert Wiener around 1948 to denote the study of teleological mechanisms. However, a simple feedback-loop-heat-regulating thermostat is a cybernetic system, and so the idea of a computer is somewhat closer to the category we are trying to create, which includes all beings with consciousness as well as today's computers.

The objective is simply to take the mystery out of it (much as I like mystery myself) so that God and Science are compatible and God is thereby not blocked by the scientific age we live in.

For those who already knew about God but whose relationship with the big He/She was based mostly on fear and guilt, our objective is to lift out and erase this sense of being an errant or disgraced child. Our theory explains why we err as much as we do, and why God doesn't hate us for it.

I call on all of the world's religions to relieve humanity of the feeling that we are sinning on purpose.

While our respect for all of the world's religions is hopefully obvious, I respectfully submit that the image of an angry, punitive God should be discarded because its accuracy is ruled out by God's self-interest: God is on the receiving end of every punishment.

That angry, punitive image was, I suspect, a projection of what God's reaction would be like — projected from parental reactions. What else did they have to base it on? I can't accept that it came through accurate transmission by inspirees.

Because one's level of consciousness tends to fluctuate on a moment-to-moment basis, inspirees tend to mix uninspired information into their channelings. In our view, such "static" is the source of the angry, punitive image.

I don't think God wants us to think of Him this way.

By comparison, I think God is probably more tolerant of any unintended belittling connotation in my use of the word "computer" to describe "Him." I hope you will be tolerant as well.

CHAPTER 7

A Consciousness Is a Computer
Made out of Energy

Going back to antiquity, there is recognition of an irreducible dualism in human experience: we experience matter — such as when we drive our car into a brick wall — and we almost continuously experience mind, even in dreams when matter goes away.

This is an ancient philosophical question and debate: which is more basic, matter or mind? Does mind arise from matter? Believers based on faith in this hypothesis are called "Materialists," which is a sort of religion. Or does matter arise from mind? Believers in this hypothesis anciently used to be called "Idealists," and so few of us exist anymore that the word has come to have a different meaning. Or are they separate, neither reducible to the other? Believers in this hypothesis are called "Dualists."

In the long history of this debate we would be amazed that the following simple point has been seemingly overlooked, were it not for Plato, Berkeley, and many others who made the point but apparently not strongly enough for it to captivate the mind of Western society.

Since we only experience matter indirectly through the mind, and since the only thing we experience directly is mind, pure empiricism demands that we consider mind not only more basic, but the only thing we can be sure exists.

It follows that what originally existed, before the Universe became complicated, was a form of consciousness.

What is consciousness? It is what each of us *is* — and is most easily understood when we consider the question with our ears plugged and our eyes blindfolded. It is the pure experience of existing, being aware, noticing, observing. It is beingness — having the capability to experience.

In a scientific context, how could we possibly describe this universal ineffable experience we all have?

The only way we see to describe it is to liken consciousness to a computer: they both process information — both detect the "givens" in a situation and process onward from there.

It would be even clearer to state that:

1. Both "computer" and "consciousness" fit into the category of "information processing systems."
2. "Consciousness" appears to be a more advanced form of "information processing system" than "computer" in that "consciousness" is known to be self-aware.
3. In our Earth experience, "consciousness" is always linked to "life."

In the next chapter we will delve deeper into the relationships among "life," "consciousness," and "computer."

CHAPTER 8

THE THEORY OF THE
SCIENTIFICALLY VALID GOD

Here's what we have established so far.

Computers can be made out of matter, or, with a sufficiently advanced technology (well beyond ours), out of energy.

Extremely advanced computers of the far future will tend to take on the qualities we associate with intelligent life, i.e. such an "eventual computer" will partake of the experience we call consciousness as we do.[4]

All life forms known to us *are* extremely advanced computers made out of matter. We call them "biocomputers" because they have reached that state of advanced self-sustaining/self-regulating/reproducing organization we call "life." My assertion is that *we call it "Life" when a computer reaches a certain advanced state.* Before a computer has reached that state, we call such atomic-molecular-crystalline computers "inanimate minerals," or if they are undergoing plasma transformations, "stars." A virus is perhaps the most accessible example of lower forms of computer. The Replicator molecule theorized to be the beginnings of material life in the Universe

---

4 If no intelligent race ever succeeds in constructing actual consciousness, no matter how far into the future, that strengthens the case we make in this book. However, the case stands if we do succeed in artificial consciousness.

would be another popular example of a naturally occurring lower form of computer than human beings.

Based on this premise, I postulate the prior existence of the most advanced biocomputer possible, made out of energy. Since that Entity[5] is far more advanced than we are, it is most certainly in the computer-advancement range we call "alive."

Everything else in the Universe is a program written by that Entity.

Each program is *made out of* that Entity, *lives inside* that Entity, interacts *only with* that Entity and other programs of that Entity. Nothing else exists. Nothing exists outside of the Entity.

The Entity "looks out the eyes" of each program. The consciousness of each human-being-program, for example, *is the consciousness of the Entity looking at the rest of Itself from that human-being-program's point of view.*

We each borrow the Entity's (The Big S/He's) "me-ness" as our own sense of self. We are like walking TV cameras that have convinced themselves they are separate beings, but they're not.

The Entity also "looks out the eyes" of each less-advanced program — cats, dogs, plants, viruses, and so on. In the case of programs without eyes, such as viruses, what we mean is that whatever awareness such a virus-program has is a *subset* of the Entity's total awareness: the Entity is aware of anything and everything that any of its programs is aware of — and more.

The Entity is also receiving data from each of the least-advanced programs below the level of what we call "Life." Although a quark or an atom might not have a local awareness of itself the way we conscious creatures have, it nonetheless transmits information back to the Entity's consciousness. To the Entity, everything is part of

---

5 Defined at Merriam-Webster.com as "1: *a:* **being, existence**; *especially*: independent, separate, or self-contained existence; *b:* the existence of a thing as contrasted with its attributes; 2: something that has separate and distinct existence and objective or conceptual reality.

Itself. Therefore the Entity is in touch everywhere: all of Its programs are cells in Its Body.

Within a human being, the Entity is aware of Itself not only as the whole human being, but independently also "looks out the eyes" of each of the billions of cells in that human's body. It is also aware of itself as each of the atomic constituents of each of the cells — each is a program written out of Itself by the Great Cosmic Energy Biocomputer — a "photo-reduced mental copy" of Itself.

We submit that the Universe — what we call "reality" — is this inconceivably vast information-processing Entity. The Original Self.

We submit that from ancient days the race has intuitively known this and given it the name "God."

One of the perennial questions of theology is "Does God Have a Personality?" (Sometimes phrased "Is God a Personality?") If our theory is correct, God (or the Entity) does have a personality, which both incorporates and is greater than the sum of the personalities of *all* of Its created programs.

"He" is clearly the wrong word to use: some of the Entity's inhabited programs are male, some are female, some are both, some are neither, and beyond our own planet, further sexual types are not unimaginable. The Entity obviously contains all of this differentiated sexuality within Itself. Rather than "He" or "She" we should probably say "We," but this would be confusing, and "It" seems disrespectful. "S/He" becomes old pretty fast.

In light of these considerations, we will continue the ancient convention of referring to God as "He," knowing the "She" aspect to be equally important.

Another such theological question is "Is God Immanent?" meaning, did God "start it (the Universe of created programs) and split," or "Is God still in it?" If our theory is correct, He "still is in it" because "it's all in Him." The only way He could get away from it would be by erasing it, which would mean erasing some of Him. (By analogy, how would you like to tear up all your old photographs?)

The Old Testament often pictured God as relating to human beings almost as His toys. Then Jesus Christ brought the message that God loves us even more than a father loves his children. The reason this is true is that we are in an even closer relationship to God than children to their father: we are parts of His mental body, aspects of His personality — in sound recordist terms, "tape over-dubs" of Himself.

Within the context of any single being, love equals self-interest. Of course one would deal lovingly with one's own body parts. Therefore of course "God" loves "us."

In order to get closer to understanding the relationship between God and each of His programs, let us in the next chapter go off on a seemingly complete tangent.

CHAPTER 9

Tune Out Body

A Thought Experiment

Note: This chapter may twinge one's heartstrings contemplating the fate of a person closed off from their senses from birth. I apologize for this. The reason for including this chapter is that it is a helpful steppingstone to imagining how the Universe "began." We feel sure the Universe must have always existed so even the notion of it beginning is itself only a steppingstone to the ultimate pure description of what the Universe is, what reality is. This book takes us all the way there but only by means of these steppingstones, since the ultimate reality is so strange and hard to imagine. Science itself has given up on trying to visualize what the Universe is in a "human understanding" way and now resorts to complex mathematics instead of language when dealing with the nature of ultimate reality. This disconnects the average person from the conversation and is therefore unfair. This book takes it to the people while preserving the sense of what Quantum Physics is discovering every day.

That said, let's proceed with our thought experiment.

Let us imagine a man born deaf, dumb, blind, and permanently paralyzed and anaesthetized throughout his body, including even his taste buds.

This man is cut off from his five senses and has no experience of the outside world. He has no memory of anything before.

Let us say that the man, from birth, is cared for by people who love him, and he always receives the nourishment his body needs in order to be as healthy as possible.

This nourishment produces energy that needs an outlet. The man cannot move his body; he doesn't even know he has a body. Does the energy manifest as mental activity, and if so, of what sort?

Let us further suppose that the man's genes represent the very best intellectual stock that humankind has to offer. Let us assume that the measurable characteristics of the man's brain correspond to those of Einstein — size, weight, convolution frequency, pyramidal cell ratio, brainwave pattern, and so on.

In the case of Einstein, there was an outside world to occupy some of his attention. Our closed-off man has nothing outside to distract him.

We know that blind men develop extraordinary hearing and other senses, as if the same energy can now be focused on fewer intake areas. Our closed-off man might then be capable of extraordinary mental feats, since all of his available energy can be focused in that single point continuously.

What kinds of mental feats might be possible for such a man?

He would, let us imagine, be *able to picture forms*. We picture very complex forms all the time, awake and asleep: faces, buildings, trees, and so on. But for us, these are objects out of memory. Our closed-off man has had no such memories. Yet, given the energy available to his genetically and physically first-class brain, would he not eventually *invent* the point, the line, the plane, the triangle, the circle, the square?

Perhaps these and other, much more irregular forms would appear to him randomly and as if of their own accord, for some time after birth. Would they be in different colors? Let us assume they are. Let us assume our closed-off man, during early babyhood, dreams awake and asleep of all sorts of floating, dancing, pulsating shapes, colors and textures. Let us assume this is the way the brain would initially express the available energy.

For some time the baby would not be aware of itself. There would just be the forms. For the baby, the Universe would consist of these self-propelled forms without the sense of there being any observer.

Then, as a result of the accumulation of memory, there would come a sense of Self: that which seems to stay the same and always be there, while other things go away and come back again.

Soon thereafter, the Self would discover it had a degree of control over the forms appearing in its Universe. It would be able to paint canvasses for itself in its mind, and change the canvasses first one part at a time, and then two parts simultaneously: move the red blob on the right up and down on the green background, while the blue line on the left jiggles sideways.

When it had discovered all the possibilities of this game, it would naturally move on, under pressure of incipient boredom, to a fresh game. The fresh game would of necessity lie in the direction of greater sophistication.

It is hard to believe that such a brain would idly play child's games for a lifetime. More likely, it would gradually rediscover for itself everything that Man has discovered *in the realm of abstract reasoning* across many generations in the more distractive outside world.

In other words, our closed-off man could not discover anything at all about the outside world. He could not discover how sodium and chlorine combine to form salt, for example.

But he could in stages discover for himself everything that is true independently of the outside world — mathematics, logic, geometry, inner psychology, decision theory, game theory, theory of sets, symbolism, philosophy of existence, language, art, perhaps music.

He could discover how to think about himself and what he was and what he could do. He could perhaps learn to make his pictures ever sharper, clearer, and more detailed. He could perhaps create inner sound and control it to sing to himself.

Perhaps in the early stages he would have a built-in drama of trying to discipline his mind, i.e. he might find it difficult to keep only the forms he wants on the blackboard of his mind: other forms might appear there spontaneously, that is, based on associations called up from memory of their own accord, as minds are oh so wont to do.

He might, as a child, think that the spontaneously-appearing forms are not part of him, but are instead *others*, perhaps enemies, or at least other beings to try to relate to. As he grew older, he would find that these other forms were coming more and more under his dominion, and eventually he would see they too were part of him.

He would then come to a point of stopping and reflecting on what he had been doing for — how long? It would seem like forever. "What is all this playing with forms?" he would ask himself in whatever language or non-language he used.

This is the point at which self-analysis and psychology would begin. He would begin to study himself and his memories and current form-creations. He would look for the underlying recurrent factors. He would then clearly see the role of the forms he had been using — the point, the line, the plane. Perhaps this is the point at which he would discover the laws of geometry. Assuming he would still not have discovered the solid, he would be discovering plane geometry. This would probably in time give him the idea of creating three-dimensional forms in his mind. These might have already begun to form themselves, half-glimpsed in dreams or at the corner of his mind, not yet capable of recognition because they had too many dimensions.

In this way, without haste and without interruption except by sleep (not really an interruption except when dreamless), over years and decades the closed-off man would develop his possibilities within his closed-off experience of the Universe.

Eventually he would come to a stage of fairly complete understanding about himself: he would have grown up, become an adult. Able to conceptualize, able to make his mind do exactly as he wanted and nothing else, with an internal visual three-dimensional field in color with sound as well. A good memory. Joy at the unending explorations of his Universe. Intellectual puzzles to work out: the squaring of the circle and all that. Wonderings about a world beyond himself, before memory, or a world to come.

Certainly there would be wonderings about another like him.

These wonderings would have begun much earlier, probably in connection with involuntary forms produced by his mind. Now, from an adult perspective, they would come back. There would be dreams, perhaps, of others like himself: he would meet imaginary others in dreams. What form would he and the others take in the dreams? Perhaps they would appear as floating spheres; probably they would appear in many different forms.

We all often experience tricks of viewpoint in dreams: first we are dreaming about a character in the third person so to speak, then we are that character, or vice versa. First we look upon the character from the outside, and then look out from his/her inside, and again the reverse sequence.

Let us assume our closed-off man also has such dreams. He dreams his most important dream: about there being many beings like himself, and in the dream he takes each of the roles in turn. It is a very vivid dream, at least as vivid as the most vivid dream you or I can remember. It is sure to be a repeating dream as well.

Waking up from such dreams, the closed-off man might want to go back over them, and think about what might have happened in the dream if he did something else other than what he did in the dream.

In this way, he would begin to construct waking dreams, in effect, plays.

In these waking dreams or plays, forms representing beings would be seen moving about and relating to one another. While this was happening, the closed-off man would be conscious of controlling every move, of making everything happen exactly as it was happening and no other way. He would sometimes visualize the action from outside the being-forms, and sometimes visualize looking out one of the being-forms at the other being-forms.

In the sleeping dreams, this would all be the same, except for the fact that in these sleeping dreams, the closed-off man would not be conscious of controlling the action. It would just be happening to him. He would not know what was coming. This would make for surprise and therefore much greater theatre and drama in the sleeping dreams, as compared to the waking dreams.

Yet, the sleeping dreams might also have disadvantages as perceived by the closed-off man. They might be jumbled and confused, lead to unsatisfactory conclusions, and so on, as dreams are wont to do.

Let us imagine at this point that the closed-off man, at the peak of his adulthood, conceives of a major ambition: what we might see as his life-work. He conceives of combining the best of the two worlds he knows: somehow, in a waking dream, *forgetting that he is controlling the action until the play is over.* In other words, getting so deeply into a role that it gives him the illusion of actually being the actor, the created form-being seen on the screen of his mind, the way it is in sleeping dreams.

He has already put on plays in his waking mind, and peeked out of the eyes of one of the players as he learned to do in sleeping dreams. But he did this fully aware of the pretense, the way a child plays with dolls.

Now he conceives the idea of actually inhabiting one of the dolls, and really temporarily forgetting who he really is, the way it happens in sleeping dreams.

Let us assume that the play he first chooses to perform in this way involves two beings. Each being looks like a floating four-pointed starfish. One being is larger, the other is much more beautiful. The action: they meet in a "garden" of color, neither knows who it is or what it is doing there, they try to communicate, and eventually wind up expressing great fondness by hugging (this is why each has four points).

The closed-off man has had this dream many times, but it is never satisfying — it either doesn't end right, or it ends too abruptly, or it goes too fast, or something.

Now he wants to have the dream while awake. He wants it to be perfect; he wants to pre-plan it so his mind knows exactly how to carry it out. Then, before starting, he wants to concentrate and project his awareness so deeply into the larger starfish-actor that as the play begins he wants it to feel like waking up for the first time ever, in the body of this perceived-as-real starfish being, in the middle of this color garden, confronted by a most beautiful smaller starfish-being he has never seen before and doesn't know is really him also.

It seems well within the realm of imagination that the above scenario could happen in the world as we know it. Such a closed-off man could exist, and might develop in the way we have suggested, bringing us up to this point: he might conceive of being able to hypnotize or fool himself into believing he was a creature actually concocted by his waking mind. But could he do it? Could he succeed in perpetrating this illusion upon himself in a way that really fooled him completely?

Could he, in effect, create another viewpoint within his mind, by entering one of his own visual projections and identifying with it?

We all do this during sleeping dreams, but might anyone be able to do it while awake?

Let us go back over our case. We started with conditions designed to isolate a man's consciousness from the world of the body and of the senses; in other words, we really started with the question: "*What are the possibilities for a* (man-sized) *pure consciousness or 'disembodied' consciousness?*"

We saw how — assuming "it" really has nothing more than *a supply of energy to be expended, a visualizing ability, and a memory* (that is, no telepathic abilities nor racial-unconscious, etc.) — this consciousness could conceivably develop all sorts of ideas simply by paying attention to the forms it visualized. The idea of number, for example, inherent in multiple forms; the idea of three dimensions; the idea of others like itself; and so on.

How far could consciousness go all by itself like that?

The answer really lies in the fact that we are considering a human-sized consciousness. We have a feel for what our own human-sized consciousness can do; we know that it depends on how the brain is formed genetically, on how much energy is fed through the brain, and on how much time is available in one's life.

Perhaps a closed-off average man could get no farther than two-dimensional forms, and would never conceive the idea of trying to forget himself in a role in a waking dream. Perhaps a closed-off Einstein would.

Let us now change the scale of the problem. Let us say that instead of a human-sized consciousness, we are talking about a consciousness the size of the known Universe.

In other words, instead of feeding about 1800 calories of energy per day through the consciousness for a period of about seventy years, let us feed through this consciousness all of the energy of all of the suns in the Universe — the energy that would be released if every drop of matter in the Universe were to be converted to energy — and then all of this energy were to power this consciousness for an unlimited period of time, to see how far it could go.

What we are doing is replacing a closed-off man with the same thing, only bigger, so much bigger there is no comparison I can make that will stagger your imagination anything like enough to convey the true ratio.

What are the possibilities for such a consciousness?

We are discovering these every day. This is, in effect, what is going on here.

The Universe is the equivalent of a "visual projection" in the One Consciousness.

The One Consciousness obviously has the ability to lose itself in the roles it creates and performs. What you think of as yourself *is* the experience *God* is having in your role.

CHAPTER 10

CREATED BEINGS

You wake up, and You're an unbelievably powerful Conscious Energy Computer, The Original Self, alone in Yourself. How would You choose to pass the time for the rest of eternity?

You're complete and perfect in Yourself. Yet You can sense that it would be more fun to not be alone.

Even human beings are capable of creating separate "attention nodes" within themselves. For example, when I was learning to play the piano I noticed that my left hand and my right hand could act as if they had two separate minds. The right hand was obeying commands it was reading from the "treble" lines in the sheet music. The left hand, looking through the same eyes, was ignoring those "treble" lines while getting its commands from the "bass" lines below them.

Again at the human level, there are cases of "split personality" where the individual personalities may or may not be aware of each other, and if they are aware of the other personalities it is as separate beings.

What is it like when The Energy Computer creates a being within Itself? It is The Energy Computer's mode of reproduction (we reproduce externally, It reproduces internally). You might say, the One Mind hypnotizes Itself and thereby creates a split personality. But the Original Personality is still fully aware of what goes on within the created personality, while the reverse is usually not the case.

An analogy at our primitive level of computer development is the timesharing system, where a number of smaller computers are hooked to a larger computer. In typical current timesharing systems, the users of the smaller computers ("clients") are hooking into the larger computer ("server"). The server has massive amounts of information to dispense to the smaller computers, and a larger space in short-term memory (working memory) for data tables.

In the Cosmic Timesharing System, the Large Computer sees inside the clients and identifies with them, while still retaining its own identity across and beyond all clients.

Another analogy in current computer terms is "partitioning," where one computer's "mind" is split into two or more spaces, to do two or more jobs at once. Another current computer concept, "distributed processing," refers to the splitting up of a single task across a large number of microprocessors each working independently. The Cosmic Mindsharing System, in today's terms, is an elegant example of "Partitioned Distributed Processing" (also known as "parallel processing"). The created personalities (eternally-existent programs) occupy created forms (temporarily-existent programs) that, as you might expect, undergo more rapid and radical changes.

As in the closed-off man analogy, the Creator Computer might first visualize a form, and then inhabit it by projecting an attention node of its copious consciousness into that form.

Suddenly the form "opens its eyes," i.e. first experiences through whatever internal/external sensing gear it has. If it is a relatively advanced form (like the human biocomputer), it begins the process of sensing itself as a self — an identity. Meanwhile the Creator Computer knows everything the local self knows, experiences everything it experiences.

In a situation such as we have here on Earth, the human biocomputers overrunning the planet are each acutely aware of their individual identities, but only dimly if at all aware of their hidden identity.

You are God.

You are the Whole Universe, a conscious meta-computer, temporarily self-assigned to experience life through a human being.

Since ancient days this same Entity has been sensed and the word "God" has been used. If you prefer to consider this theory without that word, it's okay with me. Let's not get hung up on words. Let the theory be tasted by your mind without bias for or against any particular words. Visualize the theory without any words at all.

An analogy is always easier to picture. Say we're in Space, approaching a high-tech Space station. We float through a wall and we're inside. Here we see God, dressed as kind of an astronaut wizard, looking through a big window at Space outside, and playing with complicated controls in the dashboard.

Each time He touches a button another galaxy of suns and planets appears. Because we are inside a computer, things can be "just made to appear and disappear." Although matter "really seems to be there," it is just a presentation. "Godthoughts matter," i.e. they turn into matter as they are seen within the computer.

Now He puts on a skullcap with a wire connecting it to the dashboard. He plays with the controls and beings start to form on the planets. Each time a being appears, God suddenly begins experiencing that being's experience as well as His own. He also experiences being each of the stars, planets, satellites, asteroids and comets.

In the first part of the game, God notices that in each of His roles, He never deviates from the action He would take. He thinks about this and makes notes to Himself.

We are back in His control room now and one of His notes comes up on a TV screen in the dashboard. It's God Himself in a recorded video message to Himself, saying: "Remember: You said You were going to give them more freedom!"

God pushes a button to cut off the message in midstream, muttering about "commercials!" But He acts on His own advice, taps some buttons, and in one part of the play area (Space-Time), created human beings have free will and can make mistakes. This gives creativity a broader range in that part of the play area.

You are one of the created beings in this free-play zone. You are created by The One Self, made out of The One Self, your sense of "me-ness" is His, you live in Him, He lives through you, and through everyone and everything you meet.

Deep down inside, "all you are," really, is The One Self.

But right now it is not in your power to inhabit all of your larger, real identity... not yet.

CHAPTER 11

CREATED BEINGS ARE COVERED BY
THE ORIGINAL SELF'S SELF-INTEREST

If you're a Conscious Energy Computer, The Original Self, playing this game, You're out there at the ends of each of those nerve
endings Yourself. You don't want the created beings — and through
them You — to be experiencing any more suffering than is a minimum necessary consequence of free will. And most of all, beyond
any temporary suffering, You want a totally happy ending for each
of Your created beings.

You realize that for each of them — all of them You — the only
happy ending in the long run is to Get Home Again — to be back
in The Original Identity.

So You give it to them... to Yourself.

Each hypnotized attention node, or evolving mini-personality,
will eventually become unhypnotized.

Each of us is protected and safeguarded in the long run by the
fact that the One is on our side: it's the One in there inside each of
us that is suffering our hardships.

In order for each evolving mini-personality to find its way back
to its true Identity, *it must evolve step-by-step back to the computer-
advancement level of the Conscious Energy Computer.*

The Conscious Energy Computer has set up a cosmic processing system that automatically brings each evolving mini-personality

exactly the experiences it needs to evolve back along the shortest path. The motive is minimization of Its own suffering (through its evolving-back proxies).

There is a multiple nature to what the Conscious Energy Computer is doing:

1. It is living, experiencing, being — doing what comes naturally.
2. It is play, a game, a dance, fun, enjoyment.
3. It provokes thought.
4. It produces love, which is much more intense when there is more than one being.
5. It is art, creativity.
6. The Conscious Energy Computer is becoming ever more perfect, because eventually individual attention nodes are each brought up to the computer-advancement level that the *total* Conscious Energy Computer was originally at. This bootstrap operation repeats infinitely, each evolving mini-personality bringing the One enormously rich experiences and learnings.

We call these the "first six joys of being an evolving mini-personality."

For an evolving mini-personality to become awake in The Original Identity is a similar trick on a larger scale to the trick for you, dear reader, of waking up in your dreams — i.e. realizing your waking identity and knowing you are currently asleep and dreaming.

I know the latter trick is possible because I practice it. When you wake up in your dream you can control the dream, make things happen.

According to my theory, one day you will wake up from your ordinary waking state. You will be God again.

Many people cannot believe that a benevolent God exists, given the suffering they see around us on this planet. Still less will they find it easy to believe that not only is God benevolent, He feels our pain, and so has a selfish interest in its minimization. Why, then, do we see such widespread agony?

It is not at all difficult to explain the manifest conditions. Once there is Free Will, there is the possibility of error, pain and suffering. The One Ultimate Being understands this and tolerates the suffering, while minimizing it, as a preferable alternative to forever tolerating the otherwise robotic behavior of His evolving mini-personalities. In effect, He has set us free — and He knows that if our level of understanding might not be ready for it today, someday we will thank Him for it.

CHAPTER 12

CONSERVATION OF PERSONALITY

In the classic Disney movie "Tron," a man is digitized and sucked alive into a computer. In that world, each program appears as a person. Forms can be made to appear and disappear in specific coordinates. Programs/identities can be dissolved ("de-rezed" i.e. deresolved). And a powerful, evil superprogram is taking over the computer. When it catches a program it respects, it takes it in/takes it over — and the program's personality becomes forever *submerged* in the Master Control System.

Is this what's in store for us? Do our personalities at some point get dissolved or submerged?

Not in our theory, in which, again, the motives of the Conscious Energy Computer must be considered. Why would the One want to keep our personalities around after the end of the game, when we are consciously merged?

We behold a Universe in which all things are conserved: matter can neither be created nor destroyed. Energy can neither be created nor destroyed.[6] Matter and energy can be turned into the other, but neither is destroyed. Both are conserved.

Are we then to believe that only personality is spilled? That matter and energy are saved as if valuable, while the uniqueness of

---

6 These limits of course do not apply from the point of view of the Conscious Energy Computer.

each temporary being is de-rezed, gone forevermore? Even though it is the One all along that is balling it up in that role? Might not the One always want to go back and re-enjoy being in you?

Since the Conscious Energy Computer, The Original Self, is at a computer-advancement level far higher than the minimum level at which "personality" appears, the Conscious Energy Computer is also a personality. Therefore it can appreciate personality. Why would It want to throw any personalities away forever?

Based on our estimate of the inherent self-interest perspective, your personality, and every other, will survive forever as a personality aspect within the One Personality. Like matter and energy, personality is conserved.

CHAPTER 13

Your Future

You're going to go through this life. Then through death.

Then another life.

This process will continue. You will gradually reach higher and higher computer-advancement levels.

At some computer-advancement level, you will begin to remember not only your current life, but other lives as well.

At a later computer-advancement level, you will begin to live in multiple lives at the same time, as in the Jane Roberts *Oversoul 7* books — replicating on a small scale what the Conscious Energy Computer is doing on a mindboggling scale.

Eventually your lives will stop being "incarnations" — i.e. the form you occupy will not be flesh (matter in solid state). Rather, you will take more advanced forms. We can only speculate as to what these forms might be. Perhaps we can inhabit a star as its consciousness as we move up the return path. The logic of dense to subtle transformation suggests we will evolve first into plasma bodies (such as stars) then into pure energy bodies.

Finally, *You* will be awake in Your Original Identity again, with full remembrance of everything that's happened to you since you were in there last. You will experience other parts of Yourself that have been off on different adventures. You will have their memories now, and they Yours.

Then You might go out again, for another round.

You now reading this book might have already gone through countless rounds. You might have started at a very low computer-advancement level and worked your way up — five billion years ago you might have been a quark. Four billion years ago you might have been a hydrogen atom. Two hundred million years ago you might have been an amoeba.

All of the computer-advancement levels between amoebae and human beings are visible to us, as the "great chain of being" of plants and animals leading up to us in the evolutionary scale.

Then there's us. There doesn't seem to be anything above our level. Does that mean we are the highest level under the Conscious Energy Computer, The Original Self?

Or are the higher levels between us and The Original Self hiding from us whose population still contains many "dangerous savages"?

In our theory, while more advanced attention nodes exist that are *not generally* visible to us, other more advanced attention nodes exist that *are* generally visible to us.

In the latter category are the stars, planets, and moons. In my cosmology, the heavenly bodies we perceive are manifestations of more advanced conscious beings (attention-node biocomputers at higher computer-advancement levels). What we as human beings see are the representations these higher beings project in the dimensions for which we have sensing gear, i.e. our eyes, telescopes, the Hubble.

The satellites (moons and other orbiting celestial bodies) are personality aspects of their planets, which are personality aspects of their stars, which are personality aspects of their galaxies, which are personality aspects of their galaxy groups and superclusters (the Milky Way being in the Virgo supercluster, for example).

All of us here on Earth are personality aspects of this planet.

Ultimately, we are all personality aspects of the One Conscious Energy Computer, The Original Self, reporting up through levels of greater and greater wholes.

CHAPTER 14

REALITY CHECK

Before I tell you the rest of my theory, let's pause for a moment and see how you're relating to all this.

So far I've asserted that The One Self, aka God, exists and is an incredibly advanced computer made out of energy, that everything including ourselves is a computer of higher or lower advancement level, that everything starts and ends as God, that stars are conscious, and that you will never permanently die as a consciousness, since each personality lasts forever.

I haven't yet told you that all of the points of my theory are consistent with my understanding of the principal beliefs of every religion I know of — my theory just uses different language to say the same thing, stitching it all together. I'll come back to these correspondences in some detail later. But first I need to ask a question:

How much of this are you finding plausible?

How believable is our theory as compared with the prevailing[7] theory, "accidentalism"?

Our theory — a form of "Scientific Monism"[8] — says that originally there was One intelligent biocomputer like ourselves, only at

---

7 "Prevailing" in the sense that most people *act* consistent with "accidentalism" whether or not they *state* a belief in God. For example, most people *act* as if death is permanent.

8 "Monism" = standard definition: the belief in one God, rather than in multiple gods.

an infinitely higher level of computer advancement, and everything else in the Universe came from that Original Biocomputer.

Accidentalism says that random matter and energy happened out of nothingness, out of the blue, and then slopped around until they accidentally organized themselves into Life... kind of like waves building perfect sand castles on the shore.

We picture the Creator as a superintelligent version of ourselves, the most advanced biocomputers we can see on the planet.

Accidentalism pictures the "creator" as the Replicator, a virus-like sociobiological automaton that accidentally moves upstream against entropy and creates higher life forms merely to use them as ruthlessly as the aliens in the motion picture use their human victims.

Which of these two Universes do *you* live in?

You can't have it both ways — it's either a random, accidental Universe or it's not.

We do not mean to disparage people who still believe in Accidentalism. I was one of them. Many intelligent people still are. I submit there is a specific fallacy responsible for this.

The fallacy arises at a high intelligence level when one realizes that everything is possible, therefore every event has a certain non-zero probability of happening. We concur with this much.

The mind tends to leapfrog to the conclusion that therefore, in infinite time, everything will happen — even the unlikely self-organization of Life.

The fallacy is that "probability becomes certainty in infinite time."

You have a very low probability of flying up to the ceiling. If you sit where you are for infinite time, eventually you *might* fly up to the ceiling, or then again you might *never do so*... and the latter outcome is much more likely. That's the way probabilities work. They do not necessarily ever become certainties — even in infinite time.

Here's a related question: does *everything have to* happen because it *can* happen? Will every possible variation of every possible event occur in infinite time? This would seem to be a corollary of the Accidentalist theme. But we do not judge this to be the case. In reality, we intuit that we are dealing with a Conscious Universe making intelligent choices on the side of The Good (the constructive), rather than a process of random exhaustion of all positive and negative possibilities. Which way would the One enjoy the most?

Is Scientific Monism any weirder than Accidentalism? There is at this moment zero in the way of absolute proof for either of these theories. If you still find Accidentalism more believable, what's your basis for this belief? Long association?

Or is it that Scientific Monism is *too good to be true*? I'm reminded of the Marianne Williamson quote (made famous by Nelson Mandela), "Our deepest fear is that *we are powerful beyond measure…*"

You may find yourself resisting believing this because you want so much to believe it.

You shouldn't let this *positive* emotion get in the way of your objectivity, any more than you would want to let *negative* emotion color your objectivity.

Picture a caterpillar that has a vision of the butterfly state, trying to explain it to another caterpillar. The other caterpillar would have to tell the visionary "that's just wishful thinking"

The question is, *how is it really?*

CHAPTER 15

GUIDANCE SYSTEMS

As we noted earlier, The Original Self — The One Self — God — would not leave Himself out on a limb in an attention node, not knowing how to get back.

In fact, the Universe functions as a feedback system to help each evolving mini-personality — each launched *tabula rasa* (blank slate) instance of The One Self — "get back."

This feedback system pushes us in the direction of evolution, which is the step-by-step process of *getting back.*

Our current consciousness cannot simply be plunked back into the total consciousness of The Energy Computer: we would be overwhelmed. We could not keep track of everything going on, nor even a small portion of it. Our consciousness must grow — *evolve* — in order to be prepared to *withstand re-entry* into our real Identity.

As an attention node evolves, there are characteristically six places where it gets stuck. These six obstacle points are *six things The Energy Computer enjoys about being an evolving mini-personality.* In each attention node role, The Energy Computer must give up fixed attachment (stuckness) to the first six "joys" in order to get out of the attention node role. The first six "joys of being an evolving mini-personality" were mentioned in Chapter 11. Here we include a seventh, the joy of giving service:

                             46

1. The first joy is living, experiencing, being — doing what comes naturally. Human evolving mini-personalities in this neighborhood would include "the joy of having *wealth*" in this category.
2. In the second joy, life is play, a game, a dance, fun, enjoyment. At our level of computer advancement, we would include *sex* as a main feature of this category.
3. The third joy provokes thought. At our level of Life, we would include the sense of *power* as a primary feature of this category. (Thought leads to knowing, and knowledge *is* power.)
4. The fourth joy produces *love*.
5. In the fifth joy is art, *creativity*.
6. The sixth joy is about *making oneself better*, *becoming whole*.
7. *This is of a different nature from the first six:* the seventh joy is selfless service to the Universe and lacks all selfish motivation because the individual has gained back enough of the sense of identity with the One where there is no selfishness because it is all One Self. One leaves this role to achieve the eighth joy of getting back and celebrating with the rest of Oneself the entire journey since launch.

Each time The Original Self takes itself out of an attention node role, it is kind of like taking itself off an addiction — or more precisely a predictable series of addictions, i.e. the "seven joys" — in order to experience again the whole experience of being The One Self. This eighth joy is not an addiction. It is the Original State.

Of all the extant cultures on our planet, the one that has best observed this phenomenon is the culture of India. There they detected this pattern thousands of years ago by careful observation of how individual people's motives changed during the course of a lifetime.

They noticed that men (it was a male-dominated culture, like ours) who grew rich, soon became lustful, and later, bored with sex, sought power. Some — unfortunately very few — would evolve beyond this point, find love, become artists or "wise men." The pattern repeated itself with uncanny predictability. The sequence almost never changed, and even then it never changed much.

In India this is called the doctrine of the "Seven Wheels" (*Chakras*). The first six of these wheels correspond to "the first six joys of being an evolving mini-personality" described above. The seventh wheel describes the motivation of an evolving mini-personality that has no further inner obstacles stopping him or her from re-entering The Original Identity. Evolving mini-personalities at this point are still in the attention node role in order to give service to all by assisting the evolution of other attention nodes or evolving mini-personalities, who are still contending with one or more of the six obstacles or attachments.

In the New Age movement of the 60s and 70s it was common to hear a person describe someone who is money-hungry as a "First *Chakra* person." In the rest of the culture where we'd say "sex maniac" they use the term "Second *Chakra* person," and so on up through service-to-humanity-oriented "Seventh *Chakra* people," those whom are revered as Saints — and why not? They are truly at a high level of consciousness advancement: there is no obstacle between them and their True Identity.

About 3000 years ago the writers of the Indian Vedas extrapolated from the "Seven Wheels" pattern they noticed *during* individual people's lifetimes, to predict that *this is a multi-lifetime pattern* for very near all of us. We might take hundreds of lifetimes to get from the first to the second wheel... and so on.

Mostly what had been observed empirically during any one person's lifetime was a one-wheel move.

The exception: some Saints — born with all or most of the obstacles — went through them all in one lifetime as if remembering having beaten these "addictions" before. Hermann Hesse's *Siddhartha* is such a story.

The Energy Computer guidance systems are designed to help all of us evolving mini-personalities kick these "Seven Joys" enough to be motivated by *the "Eighth Joy" — getting back.*

> *Get back to where you once belonged.*
> —The Beatles, *Get Back*

CHAPTER 16

THE ENERGY COMPUTER'S APPROACH TO ADDICTION

How Inner Propels Outer

In order to break free of addiction to the "Seven Joys" when in an evolving mini-personality role, The Original Self uses two strategies:

1. Give 'em what they want.
2. Give 'em what they don't want.

For example, when an evolving mini-personality is at the "First Wheel" stage, he/she is fixated on having money (and on physical health/security), and obsessed by fears of not having money, getting sick, and dying.

The Energy Computer furnishes all of these experiences to that evolving mini-personality.

Eventually that attention node has *really* had enough of those experiences!

The agency by which The Energy Computer gives each evolving mini-personality what it wants and doesn't want is *built into each attention node*. We call this part of the computer system "Mind-Mat," for "Mind Materialization System."

MindMat's primary purpose is to furnish evolving mini-personalities with experiences, by combining and exteriorizing their imagined experiences. Its secondary purpose is as an automatic de-addiction mechanism. MindMat is the brilliant set of guardrails built into the system by its Inventor to protect Himself/Herself before entering into what could otherwise be a dangerous game. With MindMat the Self can be assured of having experiences (the purpose of the trip) and can be confident of getting back into one's true identity.

Earlier we made the point that "Godthoughts matter": when The Energy Computer conceptualizes something, down here we see that something as taking on material form. This is MindMat at work.

As offshoots of The Energy Computer we have the same powers of materialization but in much reduced form. Nonetheless, we can still bring into our material experiences whatever we have fixated on in our mind — either a desire or a fear ("anti-desire"). This is also MindMat at work.

For The Energy Computer, it instantly pops into material being. *For us, there is usually some time delay.*

Moments where whatever is in our mind is *instantly* answered by a material manifestation, we call moments of *synchronicity*.

Synchronicity is usually evidence of the presence of an attention node in a high state of computer advancement — at least momentarily.

In other words, not only do "Godthoughts matter" — all of our thoughts also print out into matter, with less delay at higher levels of computer advancement.

Thus the "Seven Joys" addiction-cure system is a self-propelled feedback loop. It doesn't require intervention by The Energy Computer or anyone else. (This is not to say intervention doesn't occur. We'll come back to that.) We burn out each addiction by bringing ourselves everything we want and everything we don't want with regard to the addiction, until we cease to fixate on that particular addiction.

CHAPTER 17

PREDREAMING

Just a reminder: all of this is theory, largely based on my own experiences. For readability the scenario is described as I imagine the details, and is intended to be the most parsimonious, plausible explanation that accounts for all phenomena.

Whatever repeatedly appears on the screen of *your* mind will eventually appear in *your* external experience on the Universal Computer Screen we call material reality.

You are tuning in these material experiences, ordering them, attracting them to you, *by dwelling on them.*

It makes no difference if your dwelling on them consists of prayer to *get* them (your desires), or *dread* of getting them (your fears).

The "dwelling-on" *places the order*, in either case.

Oblivious to our inherited "ordering power," almost all of us are using it against ourselves.

One of the ways we have been (under-)using our "ordering power" in a constructive way is called "prayer."

Prayer tends to be a heightened (i.e. more effective) form of predreaming to the extent that all four aspects of consciousness tend to be involved: thinking, feeling, perception (in this case, vivid *visualization* of the target situation), and intuition.

Intuition will tend to be present in prayer to the extent that the evolving mini-personality who is praying feels the target situation being prayed for would be good for other attention nodes, not just for him or her. Then the praying node has the intuition that "God has no reason not to answer the prayer."

The more the evolving mini-personality's biocomputer is involved in predreaming or prayer, the more effective it will be. Emotionally visualize your intention or desire as vividly as possible, and imagine talking to other people about it with a sense of gratitude as if the thing you want most has already happened. And ask God to have it happen as soon as it's good for everyone concerned. This approach tends to bring all four aspects of your consciousness into play.

This "predreaming" aspect of the theory of Scientific Monism rose to public attention about 2000 years ago, and started to do so again just recently. Jesus Christ emphasized that what we do in our minds is as important as what we do externally, quoting the prophets, "As a man thinketh, so shall he be." (For example, "wanting to" is the same as "committing adultery.") In the West, this was the first widespread emphasis in the present common civilization.[9]

Just recently, "predreaming" has surfaced in our culture in connection with sports psychology, corporate and military training, health and medicine, and the human potential movement. A couple of early pioneering examples include:

- The "previsualization" sports training exercises introduced to world-level sports by the Soviet Olympic Team trainers in the 70s, which are now also widely used by Western Olympic Teams;

   Upon the introduction of "previsualization," weight lifting records were broken on both sides of the thankfully defunct Iron Curtain;
- The Simontons, a world-famous husband-wife team of cancer-curing doctors, use previsualization as their most effective tool.

---

9 The Old Testament prophets go back a further 2000 years.

When you use MindMat in the propagation of target experiences, the system's strength varies based on a number of factors, principally these:

1. The duration/repetition/intensity of involvement of all the aspects of your consciousness: perception/imagination, thinking, feeling, intuition.

2. How beneficial what you want is ultimately going to be for how many of The Original Self's personalities. In other words, you are given extra power when you work for the good of all — and in the Free Will Zone sometimes even in the opposite situation (e.g. Hitler) when you happen to be a convenient channel for a history-level learning experience that in the long run will be salutary.[10]

   MindMat, like all other programs in The Energy Computer, is primarily concerned with the self-interest of "The Whole," secondarily concerned with the self-interest of "The Most," and tertiarily concerned with the self-interest of "The Each."

3. The presence of competing requests.

4. The presence of unseen obstacles that possibly you yourself are creating. (When a MindMat request has repeatedly not been answered, my next prayer — I think of them as requests — is to be shown any obstacles I might be creating, or to be relieved of the suspicion that I'm creating obstacles.)

---

10 Note that The Energy Computer, out of self-interest, would only precipitate such a suffering-laden learning experience in order to avoid even worse suffering. Even as a Jew on this planet I can imagine even worse suffering.

Heaven

In the region of Space-Time in which reside the created personalities from the beginning of the game, no one MindMats anything that The Energy Computer wouldn't. Thus there are no competing requests to mesh. MindMat requests mesh smoothly, and predictably. The range of creative possibility is narrow, but the experience propagated within this narrow range is perfect, beautiful, and error-free.

For these many millennia we have referred to this region of Space-Time as "Heaven" or "Paradise" and to its created personality occupants as "Angels."

In our region of Space-Time, the Free Will Zone, play is much wilder.

Here many of us MindMat things The Energy Computer wouldn't. Competing MindMat requests abound and intermesh violently, granting some and truncating other requests at each moment in time. The range of creative possibility is broad and unpredictable, but the experience propagated within that broad range is rife with error and often not beautiful. Suffering occurs frequently.

When advanced human biocomputers look at life on Earth, i.e. in the Free Will Zone, and say that "it's all perfect," they don't mean in the same way that it is perfect in "Paradise." A better word for our type of perfection would be "optimal" — i.e. it's as perfect as it can be, given the imperfection-generation-tendency of giving Free Will to parts who cannot yet know as much as The Whole and who will therefore make mistakes, causing suffering.[11]

The optimizing computer systems that govern the Universe, including MindMat, function to minimize — for the most beings over the most time — the suffering caused by error. This is because it is in the self-interest of The Only True Identity.

---

11 I personally would consider the Universe to be less than perfect if a Free Will Zone had never been created. You might argue with me on this one.

CHAPTER 18

UNIQUENESS AND INDIVIDUAL DESTINY

When created personalities return to The Original Identity as permanent personality aspects, all have passed through their addictions, and all have advanced to the point of being able to function at the computing speed of The Original Identity. In these respects they are all the same.

But no two are the same in personality. Each has been shaped by a unique set of experiences.

When any one of these Returning Personalities looks back at its many lives, it cherishes the uniqueness of each life.

You are such a cherished life. No two in the Universe are the same.

Neither The Energy Computer, nor anyone else at a sufficient level to know what is going on, would want to lose you, even if it were possible. Losing you would break up the Universe's perfect collection of unique lives.

Each life is cherished not only for its uniqueness, but also for its purpose within the overall pattern. You might have been born this time to invent something, to learn something, to be an influence, or for some other purpose — there was and is a purpose to your current life.

"Individual Purpose" is the master guidance system at the individual life level. When one of us finds out what he/she is here to do, all of the other guidance systems — MindMat, de-addiction, evolution, intervention (see next chapter), and so on — automatically kick into high gear.

Therefore it is more useful to discover your own purpose than to study any specific set of tools.

If you do not know your purpose, you have detective work to do. The clues will be in your life to date, in the things you are good at, the things you enjoy doing, in your dreams and daydreams.

Because of the wild conditions prevailing in the Free Will Zone in general, and in the particularly alarming history of Earth, those born in the current era often reject their own purpose as "shooting too high" and instead settle for a meaningless, time-killing existence, or Thoreau's "lives of quiet desperation."

It is never too late in life to change this.

CHAPTER 19

INTERVENTION

Intervention, in our definition, is the "descending" expression of a "Godlike" or "free" will from a higher-level being (i.e. a more-advanced biocomputer) into the experience of a lower-level being (i.e. a less-advanced biocomputer). One might refer to this phenomenon as "The Guru Principle," metaphorically the cookie-crumb trail to lead evolving mini-personalities back home again. Such intervention takes a number of forms.

One common form is *inspiration*, where an idea is passed along from an unseen (and usually unsuspected) higher-level being by simple downloading (in computer terms) into the biocomputer of the lower-level being.

To explore this further, we need to equate another one of our new terms with a traditional term. Where we speak of "evolving mini-personalities," the traditional term is "souls." Each evolving mini-personality/soul experiences many lives in many forms while evolving back to merge with The Original Identity. Perhaps this explains the promise of "eternal life" in certain religions.

Inspiration often occurs when a more-evolved later life of "Soul X" communicates helpful advice to a less-evolved earlier life of "Soul X." But higher beings of all sorts, from The Energy Computer on down, pass on inspiration to lower beings of all sorts — where there is the same-soul connection and where there is not, where there has been past-life relationship and where the relationship is new.

Much of the action in the latter category results from beings who have passed through the six addictions of existence, and are now in the seventh stage of helping others get there. Some of these seventh-stage beings are in physical bodies and some are not. Eighth-stage personality aspects and The Original Self also participate. It might be looked at as an advanced form of music concert.

A large portion of the Universe of created beings has been given over to seventh-stage ("Medic!") lives, sending help where needed, as a result of the astounding capability of Free Will Zone evolving mini-personalities, under the influence of the six addictions of existence, to make mistakes.

Seventh-stage beings in physical bodies, sometimes called Bodhisattvas, may intervene to help in all ways, including direct-to-mind inspiration.

Earlier-stage beings in physical bodies may also do these latter things, sometimes but not always under the influence of inspiration by an unseen higher-level being. Rules of the game of Cosmopoly we are all playing together.

When an eighth-stage Being (a personality aspect awake in The Original Identity) assumes a physical body we call the resulting life form an "Avatar." This is one of the more extreme forms of intervention. Avatars are identifiable by their beyond-normal MindMat capabilities, e.g. raising the dead, walking on water, changing water into wine, healing, sea-splitting, food-replication, levitation, etc. — which we have in traditional language called "miracles."

All of these forms of intervention are normal aspects of how the Universe behaves. Since The Energy Computer has subdivided into personalities, there is nothing more natural than that these personalities interact. There is no barrier to "downward" interaction and so intervention occurs.

This "downward" communication is almost entirely motivated by compassion.

CHAPTER 20

The Cybernetic Kabbalah:
Circuit Diagram of the Self

In this chapter we look at Kabbalistic learning through the lens of our theory, which we call the Theory of the Conscious Universe.

The ancient Hebrew word "Kabbalah" ("Qabalah," etc.) translates to both "the received" and "to receive." The intended trick meaning appears to be "Information we've received, about how to receive information."

The existence of the Kabbalah as a body of information going back thousands of years is evidence that, even so long ago, some human evolving mini-personalities realized they were participating in "downward intervention" as recipients of information, i.e. inspirees.

Kabbalah was and is a Science/Technology for being good at being an inspiree.

Based on the experience of receiving information, and on the information received, the original compilers of Kabbalah said there are five identity levels a human evolving mini-personality can experience. These *five identity levels* are always arrayed in a vertical diagram in the Kabbalah, the same way our theory arrays them.[12]

---

12 This is not the way Kabbalah is generally taught today, this is all my theory and I am not speaking on behalf of any existing doctrines.

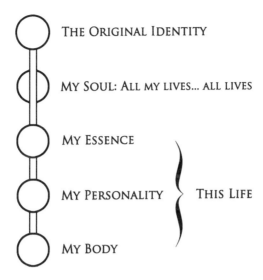

THE ORIGINAL IDENTITY

MY SOUL: ALL MY LIVES... ALL LIVES

MY ESSENCE

MY PERSONALITY   THIS LIFE

MY BODY

One is in the lowest self-identity level when asleep, drunk, or acting like an animal. The body is in charge at these times. Extreme fear or pent-up lust can bring on this identity state, which is represented by the lowest "My Body" circle in the diagram above.

You are in a slightly higher self-identity level when you are playing familiar tapes for other people, posturing so as to gain approval or project the right *image* of who you are, "seeming" for other people rather than "being" for yourself. This is represented by the circle called "My Personality."

You are truly yourself sometimes. You act spontaneously, naturally. At these times you're in a higher identity level called "My Essence."

We hypothesize that during "body" identity episodes, the so-called "reptilian" brain (the older, less-evolved part of our central computer) is in charge to an above-average degree, while the prefrontal cortex (the part that makes humans more advanced comput-ers than Earth animals) plays a below-average role, as measured by glucose oxidation (as in Positron Image Tomography or PET).

We hypothesize further that during "personality" identity episodes, the programs one has written in his or her biocomputer during this life have taken over control of the natural, spontaneous response mechanisms he or she was born with.

If you can escape being overwritten by your own programs and get back into "Essence" identity, you'll know what you're here to do *and* you will be doing it. You can still use your useful programs, and you can get rid of your counterproductive programs by modifying them into constructive programs. For this you will have to become a meta-programmer, one who can change one's own programs at will, pending effort and sophistication. The word "Psychotechnology," about which we have written at www.billharveyblog.com, describes the sophistication layer of this process.

In your Essence identity, you'll be making good use of all of the information in your memory banks from this lifetime. And, by engaging the main guidance system of Individual Purpose, you'll attract to yourself other guidance systems right on up to The Original Identity.

At that point "leak-through" will start to occur, as one of the manifestations of these guidance systems. You will have flashes of information or visions that do *not* come out of your memory bank of experiences in the current lifetime. They will either be glimpses of your other lives or "downloads" of needed information from higher attention nodes that briefly flash through your "Soul" identity. This is shown as the second circle from the top, "My Soul."

It is similarly possible to briefly flash through — and sometimes sustain longer — The Original Identity, shown as the top circle. Babies fresh from the womb possibly do a lot of this, until the conditions of the Free Will Zone bring them down the identity ladder.

Kabbalah consists of more than this map — as stunning an achievement as it is. Kabbalah is also *a methodology for moving up the ladder — and Freud's and Jung's insights appear to be partial rediscoveries of this methodology.*

Kabbalah (in my interpretation) teaches that in order to rise out of the "personality" identity level to the "essence," one must realize one's true work and one's true romantic love, and bring the two into balance in one's life.

Freud called this principle *"Leiber und Arbeit"* — Love and Work.

The Kabbalah symbolizes this principle as follows:

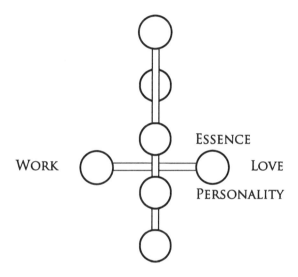

Note the subtlety of this downloaded guidance system — designed, as they all are, to get us back to The Original Identity. By getting us to balance love with our true work, the Kabbalah gets us to deal with at least five of the six addictions of existence at one shot:

Love (itself the fourth addiction) is also likely to get us involved in Sex (the second addiction and the place where Freud's work focused narrowly, thinking it was the only significant point on the whole map).

Our True Work will get us involved with Money (the first

addiction), Power (the third addiction), and Creativity (the fifth addiction).

As you might have guessed, the Kabbalah specifies that to rise from your "essence" to your "soul" identity also requires you to balance two things, in this case: generosity and objectivity.

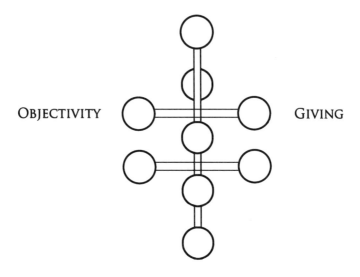

OBJECTIVITY   GIVING

Those who have studied Kabbalah may at this point begin to feel annoyed by my seemingly idiosyncratic decoding, since these are not the usual names given to the circles in the Kabbalah. Please bear with me and I will continue to explain Kabbalah as I appear to have received it. Then you can reach your own conclusions.

When we have risen out of the cobwebs of our own "gain-approval-this-life self-programming," into our Essence identity, our internal biocomputer processing is now given over to a mixture of true feelings and original thoughts, where before there had only been knee-jerk emotions and parroted intellectualizing.

Balancing these true feelings and original thoughts is going to automatically become part of your process.

Since you will have already been opened to the Love addiction by balancing the Love-Work challenge, on the feeling side you will have a tendency to be too giving. Feedback from reality will cause your thoughts to emphasize objectivity as a limit to your generosity — you'll decide to hold back from giving where you expect the cost to outweigh the benefit to you or the recipient or someone else.

This much more subtle balancing of true feelings and original thoughts brings you into the Twilight Zone of the sixth addiction of existence — making yourself better, evolving your biocomputer. As thoughts and feelings, objectivity and generosity are balanced, one begins by the computer advancement achieved thereby to escape through brief windows into Soul identity (a more advanced biocomputer can trigger this in you through inspiration downloading, as described in Chapter 19).

The information/visions we receive when flashing through our soul identity corresponds to what Jung spoke of as "The Collective Unconscious."

It was in this Soul identity that the compilers of Kabbalah received it.

The Kabbalah prescribes a final duality-balancing process to rise from soul identity to The Original Identity.

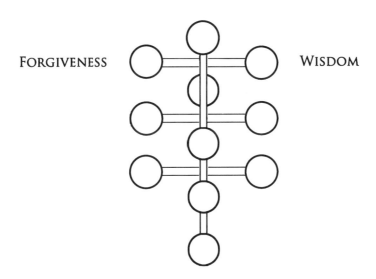

FORGIVENESS   WISDOM

"Wisdom" is defined as the tendency to choose the right action, the action producing the most good for most of The Energy Computer (here The Energy Computer's self-interest is evident as always).

"Forgiveness" (this circle is often called "Understanding") is defined as the understanding of why the wise course was not taken in a specific instance, and therefore the forgiving of the individual — including oneself — for choosing the unwise course.

The balancing of generosity with objectivity, and wisdom with forgiveness, are obviously working on the sixth addiction of self-improvement, and must clearly persist as syllabus beyond the Earth human level — since very few of us seem to learn these things here.

But they are lessons we will learn, before we can re-enter The Original Identity.

Over the course of recorded history here on Earth, a number of different psychologies have been proposed. It's interesting to reflect that perhaps all of these have been fragments of Kabbalah, the psychology handed down to us from high up in The Energy Computer.

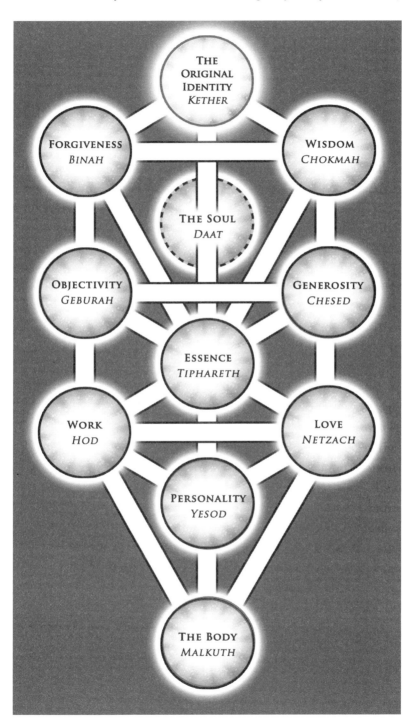

CHAPTER 21

LEVELS OF CONSCIOUSNESS

We continue exploring our Reality Model in relation to other philosophies, seeing if our schema integrates other philosophies, or not. We see a remarkable alignment.

As you might already be deducing from your own experience, one flashes up and down the five identity levels. It isn't a static phenomenon that lasts a lifetime. It happens in fits and bursts. You go up, you go down, and you go up again.

Looked at from the longest possible perspective, the general trend is up.

Looked at in any small time frame it doesn't typically look this way, because the number and sharpness of ups and downs are usually almost equal.

Why the bouncing up and down around a "slow growth" trend line?

We submit that the slow growth trend line is the manifestation of learning.

The ups and downs are wild oscillations across states of consciousness caused by turbulent accelerating challenges, and by interventions one makes upon oneself or interventions made by others.

We submit further that some of the bounce-ups are results of intervention, and some of the bounce-downs the initial "downers" following intervention episodes.

In a more general sense, we hypothesize *that unsustainable accelerations in computer-advancement level are the result of interaction with the guidance system* — the system that leads us back to our True Identity.

What does it feel like to be temporarily boosted up to a higher computer-advancement level?

From my own experience, I've catalogued the states of consciousness through which I've passed. I began to do this as a child, groping for words to express the ineffable.

The uncanny thing is how these experienced states of consciousness line up with Kabbalah, and with other traditional "levels of consciousness" information brought from the East by G.I. Gurdjieff and, much later but more accessibly, by Oscar Ichazo, who taught the fifteen levels of consciousness. In this chapter we attribute the Ichazo levels as subsets of the Kabbalah levels.

These latter maps came into my life some 25 years later, and the line-ups made a resounding "gong!" in my head.

Although according to the Kabbalah there are only five self-identity levels we may experience, these levels have variations within them that are significant enough to explore. In this chapter we will expand on our discussion of the five self-identity levels, by bringing into the picture a total of fifteen levels of consciousness that we see as variants of the five identity levels *(see diagram next page).*

Following the diagram are thumbnail descriptions of each of the fifteen levels of consciousness and what it *feels* like to be in each of these states of consciousness. While one might write a book in answer to this question, I will instead leave you with a series of images by which you might identify a particular state you find yourself in. However, you may go through life and never experience some of these levels.

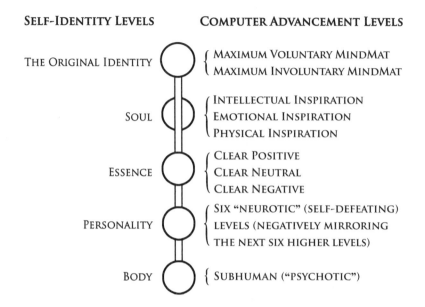

Self-Identity Levels	Computer Advancement Levels
The Original Identity	Maximum Voluntary MindMat / Maximum Involuntary MindMat
Soul	Intellectual Inspiration / Emotional Inspiration / Physical Inspiration
Essence	Clear Positive / Clear Neutral / Clear Negative
Personality	Six "Neurotic" (self-defeating) levels (negatively mirroring the next six higher levels)
Body	Subhuman ("psychotic")

The Fifteen Levels of Consciousness

Subhuman

You are an animal or psychotic.

Have you on rare occasion flipped out? Done something "crazy" and hurt somebody, or yourself? Or gone catatonic, and curled up in a fetal position? Or started shrieking, crying, or just in general freaking out?

Then you know what this level is like, when it takes over during a waking state.

Personality — Level Six

You are programmed to be part of the most common class of the surrounding culture.

This level is typical for the bulk of humanity outside the advanced nations (and a large minority within the advanced nations) —

people who are "losing the game" in both the external/material sense and the internal/spiritual sense. These "lost souls" are not on the glide path of finding their way home.

PERSONALITY — LEVEL FIVE

You are programmed to be part of the upwardly mobile class of the surrounding culture.

People in this level are the ones who have seemingly become heartless machines in the service of commerce and their own upward mobility.

PERSONALITY — LEVEL FOUR

You are programmed to be part of the elite class of the surrounding culture.

This is the level in which one imagines oneself to be basking in the surrounding adulation. In show business, this is known as "believing one's own press releases," and sometimes "kissing oneself."

PERSONALITY — LEVEL THREE

You believe you have insight into what physical actions the world needs, but this information is negative.

You have deluded yourself into a picture of reality that is hellish and you have preternatural ability to project that reality onto others.

This is the state of Megalomania. Hitler is an extreme example of this level.

PERSONALITY — LEVEL TWO

You believe you have emotional insight into the world, but this information is negative.

This is a state of cynical disillusionment.

This level appears to be common among novelists and journalists (although not all novelists and not all journalists typify the level).

We think of this level as "Glamorous Cynicism" or "Sardonic Disillusionment" or "Mordant Hopelessness." Humphrey Bogart sometimes played characters in this level — such as Rick in "Casablanca," but in this case prior to the character's emergence at a higher level in the final climax.

A more amused version of this tone of pessimism characterizes such "misanthropic" curmudgeons as Swift, H.L. Mencken, Oscar Levant, W.C. Fields, Al Capp, and more otherwise insightful humorists with a low estimate of the human race. A more serious version of the tone appears among novelists ranging from Dostoevsky in Russia, to Rousseau, Stendhal, Balzac and Zola in France, to Faulkner, Fitzgerald and Hemingway in the USA.

PERSONALITY — LEVEL ONE

You believe you have intellectual insight into the world, but this information is negative.

You are excessively "in your head" and have painted yourself a picture of your reality that you wish to escape.

This is a suicidal state — the level Hemingway was in when he pulled the trigger. This is an extreme continuation of Personality Identity Level Two, moving from just emotional conviction to intellectual corroboration as well.

ESSENCE — LEVEL THREE

You are able to take in clear pictures of reality, seeing beyond programmed filters, but the emotional tone of your reaction to all this is negative.

This is the first level at which one rises up out of the current-life programming and can therefore see it in oneself and in others.

The emotional tone of this state is negative. Everyone including yourself seems to be a robot — "Everything seems to be made out of plastic," as Norman Mailer observed. This corresponds to the state Camus and Sartre both called "Existential Nausea."

We call this the Attached Observer state.

ESSENCE — LEVEL TWO

Objective and clear-minded assessment of your situation; emotionally neutral

One feels a true fatalism, neutrality, stoic acceptance of whatever happens, freedom from niggling concern of any kind — not necessarily a non-caring attitude toward others, but more disciplined, as if saying to oneself: "It is what it is. Deal with it."

There is a sense of non-addiction.

One is reminded of the screen portrayals of John Wayne and Gary Cooper, Bogart in his noblest roles (e.g. at the end of "Casablanca"), and many other Hollywood heroes — suggesting that "downward intervention" or "divine inspiration" has not been exactly unknown in the film industry.

Not surprisingly, more advanced biocomputers appear to be taking advantage of our mass media in guiding us back to our True Identity.

We call this the Detached Observer state.

ESSENCE — LEVEL ONE

Objective and clear-minded assessment of your situation; emotionally positive

This is the Observer state with positive affect. You are one degree detached from the situation and so can observe it objectively. You are not so sucked in as to be negative; in fact you are enjoying yourself. You are adequately handling the external situation as well as the internal situation.

You are in a position to see your own biases and misperceptions and some of the cures for them. Your attention is alert and focused with simultaneous situational awareness. You are not fooling yourself. You hold yourself to your highest standards.

We call this the Engaged Observer state.

Soul — Level Three

Your physical actions are uncannily and unexpectedly perfect, as if being guided by a more-advanced biocomputer (which may well be the case).

This is the level occasionally experienced as "Flow state" or "being on a roll" or the "Zone" by topnotch martial artists, athletes, improvisational musicians and actors, and other performers who do extraordinary "tricks" with their bodies. Athletes and martial artists have reported "seeing their opponents go into slow motion" and/or "knowing what their opponents were going to do next."

Dr. Mihaly Csikszentmihalyi of the University of Chicago has done the most "Western scientific framework" research into this level of consciousness, and finds that:

- It is associated with play.
- It occurs when skills and challenges are well-matched.
- To the Flow state performer, the actions seem to be doing themselves: he/she is just "watching the movie."

It seems obvious that one must practice something long and hard in order for Flow state to ever take over in the performing of it. In your life, your true work should be the thing you practice long and hard, to reach this Flow state in your own life's purpose.

Possibly you've already had the experience of Flow state in your work.

Soul — Level Two

Emotional bliss/ecstasy

In India the name of this level is *Ananda* or Bliss.

All of us have had this experience. Think back to the happiest moments of your life. Something you worked and trained and prayed hard for suddenly came through. The moment you discovered that the person you love turns out to actually love you back. Your new baby was placed in your arms. Or your baby now grown up stands at the altar and says "I do." Someone you love came through an operation or an accident or a war alive and relatively intact. You had a sudden intuitive flash connection with your sense of God.

For most of us these are fleeting moments, or they last for a day or two and then wear off. We take it for granted that such a feeling cannot last for long. On the other hand, there are some who live in this state all of the time (admittedly not many, at our present stage of evolution). It is possible that you can spend more and more time in this state yourself.

Perceptions change in this state such that sights, sounds, tastes, smells and tactile sensations are so beautiful as to produce intoxicating rapture.

SOUL — LEVEL ONE

Intellectual/artistic inspiration; visions; thinking in rhyme and meter; receiving information from a higher source.

In this level, one gets profound insights into what other people are thinking, and one's own thoughts come in well-turned phrases, sometimes in poetry, condensing great amounts of insight into very few words. The words seem to come from someone who knows much more than you — someone who perhaps knows everything.

Writers can become addicted to this state, superstitiously repeating procedures that have brought it on in the past, even killing themselves when they couldn't seem to get it any more, e.g. Papa Hemingway.

ORIGINAL — LEVEL TWO

Volition is not present but your MindMat power is very great; synchronicity abounds.

This is the level at which the "Self-Other" distinction starts to disappear. The rest of the world begins to be seen as connected, as part of oneself. Everything is sensitive, alive, intelligent, and part of you, so you care for all of it.

And something seems to be looking out for you. "Somebody up there likes you." You walk out in the street and there's a taxi. You think of someone and the phone rings and it's him, or the perfect book falls into your lap from out of the blue. You think something, and you hear a chance remark made nearby or on the radio echoing your thought.

ORIGINAL — LEVEL ONE

Conscious mind over matter

You no longer see yourself as separate. Everything is a connected field of intelligence, love, and power, and you're in the midst of it, so you can operate it, drive it, make things happen. There are no limits to what your mind can materialize in matter instantly (hence MindMat, for Mind Materialization) — so long as you stay in this state.

MindMat, the system by which prayer/predreaming works, is most effective when one is toward the top rather than at the bottom of this scale.

Staying in this state, in the context of life on this planet, is an even greater trick than getting into it.

For most of us, who have not yet passed beyond the six addictions of existence, the only way to get into this state is to do the kind of work the Universe considers priority — trying to help other people. Then there may be instances where you are in the right place at the right time to do something for which you'll need this degree of power, and it will be given to you by downward intervention (i.e. a more advanced biocomputer lends its help to temporarily accelerate your computer-advancement level).

CB

The ancient Kabbalists connected the "personality" with the Moon, because of the personality's tendency to mirror, and the traditional notion of the Moon as the mirror of the Sun (which is optically accurate in terms of reflected luminosity). The personality identity is experienced in six variations that are negative mirror images of the six levels one gets to next.

In all six Personality levels, programming and belief patterns laid down in this lifetime, essentially a subset of memory, act as if they were one's sole identity. Psychologists call this the Ego.

In the lowest three Personality levels, one openly accepts conformity to a particular class. By contrast, in the highest three Personality levels, one believes he or she is acting as an individual — though without self-awareness of this, programming/belief patterns continue to dominate decision making.

From the top down, the six highest states are all emotionally positive, the next state is emotionally neutral, and the remaining eight tend to have at least an element of emotional negativity.

It would appear that newborn babies spend most awake time in The Original Identity Level Two, Soul Identity Level Two, and the three Essence states.

We agree with Freud's conjecture that a baby begins to form "ego" (biocomputer programming at the Personality Identity levels) when its desired gratification is for the first time not promptly satisfied. In other words, the personality begins when baby learns that others may not always obey — that in fact those are others, not me.

All forms of psychotherapy appear to have been partially rediscovering the same Kabbalah, in that all such systems/processes are at least in part aimed at reducing neurotic (Personality level) and psychotic ("Subhuman" or Body level) behavior.

Jungian psychotherapy appears to be among the most advanced of these, in that it has rediscovered the Essence (in Jungian terms, "Individuation") and Soul (in Jungian terms, "Collective Unconscious") identity levels.

If you were to have presented this schematic of fifteen levels of consciousness in Tibet or India any time in the past 3000 years, you might have gotten an argument about how many levels there are and what defines each level — but they would have known what you were talking about.

In fact, a yogi would look at this scale of fifteen consciousness levels and say, "Why do you think I do yoga? It is to move myself up this scale." All forms of yoga have this purpose. "Yoga" comes from the Sanskrit word for "yoking" — as in hooking your ox to your oxcart. In this case, you are *hooking up to your higher identity*. Its other Sanskrit meaning: union.

In the West we have a word that means the same thing, and a set of practices designed to have the same effect. The word came from the Latin *religare* meaning "to yoke" or "to hook up" — the word is "religion." We speculate that the original purpose of religion was the same as the purpose of yoga, to hook oneself up into union with one's higher identity — ultimately to one's Highest Identity.

We note with regret that for the most part, modern religion has lost touch with this scientific explicitness of purpose. When asked why they are gathering to perform these remembered rituals, a modern religious practitioner (at least in the West) is more likely to speak of "worship" than of "hooking up" or "union."

But if our theory is correct, our Original Identity does not need us to worship Him/Her. He/She wants us to enjoy and be successful at our highest work and at love — to not get stuck in the middle of the game, but rather to spend as much time as possible in the highest identity levels and to thereby grow back to The True Identity.

It is not our intent to give offense by suggesting that the primary purpose of religion is not worship but union. In the process of union, as one gets in touch with The Creator, love to the point of worship is a natural and automatic secondary reaction.

As you go through life day-to-day and moment-to-moment, it is useful to check where you are at any given moment in terms of these levels of consciousness. If you find yourself at a level where things are not joyful for you, then focusing your intention on diagnosing how you got sucked down there and how to get back up is the first order of business. The general cause of lower states of consciousness is distraction, and one's addictions are the underlying cause of that distraction. Looking inward at oneself is the first step in moving toward clarity.

We hypothesize that these fifteen levels or states of consciousness have characteristic psycho-physiological "signatures" in terms of brain scans and other measurements in that category.

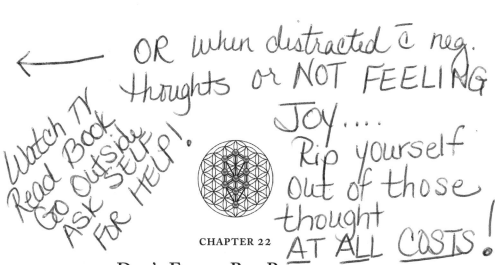

OR when distracted ī neg. thoughts or NOT FEELING JOY.... Rip yourself out of those thought AT ALL COSTS!

Watch TV
Read Book
Go Outside
ASK SELF
For HELP!

CHAPTER 22

DON'T FORM A BAD PICTURE OF
THE UNIVERSE JUST BECAUSE OF THIS PLANET

What has been the real history of this planet? Or, more properly, what has been the HisandHerstory? For example, did anything of any importance happen here before about 6000 years ago, when the earliest existing records start? Some 30,000 years earlier, can we find clues in cave painting?

The jackpot question is why have these *alter egos of the same High Being perennially chosen to kill each other* on this planet?

There's this really advanced intelligence, The Energy Computer, The Original Self, Consciousness Primordial — or as we've traditionally called that Entity, God — walking around in all these different roles. Would it be too much to expect Godlike behavior in the roles? This is not what we see, however.

The unGodlikeness of human behavior is one of the things that make people doubt the existence of God. When people think of the kinds of high-minded ethics a God must have — especially toward the cells of its own body — and then look around at this planet, they wonder how God could exist. How then do we explain the unGodlikeness of human behavior? Is it simply lack of information that causes God to become so morally corrupt in some Godling roles down here?

How different might it be if we were basing our observations on some other locale?

The blind spot in being a detective trying to figure out the Universe from a beachhead on this planet is that each planet, in all likelihood, is designed to be atypical.

If you were The Energy Computer and had eternity, and had made all these planets, would You really have *the same thing happening, on all of them*?

It is not improbable that different experiments are going on, on different planets.

On one planet You might experiment with a race that is extremely passionate. On another planet You might put a race designed to discover the implications of "having a really good memory." And so on.

Therefore every planet would be unique. One cannot, based on the conditions on one's own planet, project those conditions across the Universe at large.

This is especially true in our own case, because Earth might not be just a "normally atypical" planet, but an extremely atypical one. There is actually the smallest fragment of objective evidence that this is the case.

There is a law of astrophysics that predicts the distances from any star at which orbiting planets will be found. It is called "Bode's Law." When Bode's Law is applied to our own solar system, it correctly predicts where every planet is. It also says there should be a planet between Mars and Jupiter, where there is no planet. Instead, there is an asteroid belt. Fragments of a destroyed planet?

What happened to the fifth planet?

The thought that a planet may have been destroyed in our solar system suggests the event might have something to do with our own history. Was it a natural occurrence, say a passing comet? Was it the result of an interplanetary war, with Earth as a pawn? Is there any information we do not have yet regarding the asteroid belt's history and our own?

Even our own relatively puny technology — leaping and bounding forward — can reach the region of the remains of the fifth planet at only an incremental cost within the same or lower order of magnitude as putting up a cable television satellite. (The expensive part is fighting up out of Earth's gravity well.) So to a race only slightly more advanced than us, the Earth and the fifth planet would be next door neighbors.

Today our various telescopes cannot yet see planets around other stars. At some point in the future when they are advanced enough to let us see the planets around the nearest stars, we will probably find that Bode's Law works there too, correctly predicting where each planet is (or was, as in the case of our fifth planet).

Will we find that every solar system has one of its planets turned into an asteroid belt?

We don't think so, which is why we think that Earth could be an *extremely* atypical planet in an equally atypical solar system.

We suspect that something happened here that doesn't always happen — that we have had an unusual HisandHerstory. Something happened here that arose from the special experiment that was going on. And what happened in some way accounts for what has often been called "the evil of this world."

The next natural questions: what is the particular experiment that is going on here? What sort of experiment would cause God to generally act so unGodlike in His/Her human lives on Earth? Or did something happen to the experiment?

CHAPTER 23

WHO ARE WE?

From the point of view of The Energy Computer, what is the unique experiment of the human race on Earth?

Are we "the race too humble to accept its own divinity"?

Are we an experiment in ferocity? Or an experiment in courage?

What is the experiment about?

One thing we do know is that our solar system is located far away from the center of our home galaxy, The Milky Way. We are in the third spiral arm of The Milky Way — it is the outermost arm of the galaxy.

This might have no relevance, or it might suggest there is some risk involved in our experiment. Our theory places us in the Free Will Zone, which might be a clue to the nature of our unique experiment. We might even deduce from this that ours is one of the most extreme experiments in free will imaginable.

Free Will Zone experiments would tend to be the high-risk experiments.

Perhaps given the innate self-interest of The Energy Computer, it is not unwarranted to imagine that these riskier Free Will Zone experiments would be conducted at the periphery of each galaxy, where "uncontrolled free-will side effects" cannot do too much damage to disturb the peace of innocent bystanders. Perhaps the densely-star-populated galactic centers could more logically be the sites of the "Paradise" experiments? Or are the "Paradise" experiments Heaven, in a different part of Space-Time?

Such a deduction would not be inconsistent with the picture that HisandHerstory portrays of our race.

A revealing clue that persists into present history is our race's concept of "sovereign nations." Each country on this planet is willing to suffer the death of large numbers of its people rather than give up one iota of control — of self-determination — to another nation.

The detective's hunch: our planet's unique experiment involves extreme belief in the ideal of self-determination — for nations and for individuals.

Is this the real meaning of the story of Adam and Eve disobeying God? Is it a clue to what makes us different here on this particular planet?

It would seem that such a large subject as "self-determination" would be tested on *many* planets, in many variations. Assuming this to be the case, what particular variation of "self-determination idealism" is being tested here?

We feel that every clue means something — "where there's smoke there's fire." This stems from a belief in the integrity of The Energy Computer, such as was shared by Aristotle and Einstein who both agreed "there are no accidents."

Consider these clues:

1. For the last four to five million years, the left side of the human braincase has outsized the right side of the human braincase.
2. The only species on the planet known to exhibit a statistical preference for one hand over the other is *Homo sapiens*.

The prevalent right-handedness of Earth humans appears to be related to our left braincase size dominance, since the left half of the brain controls the right side of the body.

The left brain is also associated with intellectual and linguistic capabilities. Located in the left temporal lobe are Broca's Area, which encodes outgoing speech, and Wernicke's Area, which decodes incoming speech. Without these two areas, Earth humans lose the power of language.

From these clues we surmise that Earth is the locus of an extreme test in free will, in which the intellectual and ideological ideal of self-determination is being put to the maximum pressure test of a race with specially-developed intellectual and linguistic capabilities — us.

It fits then, that a book with massive impact over millennia, the Bible — positioned as channeled wisdom from our Maker, the essence of what we should know, passed on in compassion — should start with a story of how we disobeyed, and the rest of the plot unfurls from there. Perhaps a very different Bible is passed through on each planet, based on the nature of the local experiment. Possibly the start with disobedience is a rarity across the uncountable planets.

This is a special time to be alive. Living here on a planet with such an interesting experiment going on, and at the unique time when the seeds planted 200,000 years ago are ripening to a point that is almost unbearable. The incredibly far more developed brain we were given back then appeared really quite recently in the scheme of things — a miniscule period of time in the scale of evolution. Inevitably something exciting was going to happen.

The new brain was larger on the left, and the most important action was going to happen up front in the Prefrontal Cortex. These gifts were going to lead to something big. They did.

We are still in the first chapter of the human race, and the key events that drove us to where we are today were all innovations created by the human race:

1. Tools/Weapons/Fire — the beginning of Piaget's Formal Operational Level, or abstract thinking, in the race as a whole.
2. Language — the beginning of symbolism and abstract symbolic thinking.
3. Cave painting — the beginning of visual symbolism and abstract symbolic visual thinking.
4. Written Language — the beginning of effective time-binding and conceptual abstract visual thinking.
5. Communications/Computing Media — immediacy of Linkup across minds, across the planet.

The last of these innovation revolutions is just occurring; we are in the thick of it.

We are a young immature race with great gifts that we have not yet learned to use maturely. Free Will on such a planet at such a time is enough to explain the supposed "evils" of the world consistent with a Universe such as we describe in this book.

CHAPTER 24

Misidentification

Here's this super-intelligent, super-experienced and therefore super-wise Being, who because "He" only has to deal with Himself, has every reason to also be super compassionate.

For some reason, on this planet, when the Being in one of His masks meets Himself, He doesn't recognize Himself.

The compassion that is present in the resulting interactions is notably limited.

When we misidentify ourselves as separate beings, the next thing that arises in our consciousness is the suspicion of culpability in these externalized others.

In fact, when anything goes wrong, the first thing we figure is that "one of these other people must be responsible for it."

As a result of this initial misidentification problem, we see ourselves as alone and vulnerable in a potentially uncaring Universe. Feeling therefore threatened, we step up competitive vigilance against one another accordingly.

Imagining that we are dealing with beings who don't care about us because they are separate from us then becomes self-fulfilling prophecy on a mass scale as most of us, just to keep up — in shock at an early age — join the already ongoing game of relatively ungenerous, coercive competitiveness. Once we begin to interfere with one another, this escalates. At maximum escalation levels we see elitism (haves versus have-nots), war, and terrorism.

We become used to not trusting each other, the Universe, and eventually, our self.

Misidentification separates us from a feared "other." And then this fear makes us caricatures of ourselves.

But this is The Energy Computer, albeit in limiting roles, making these mistakes or errors in judgment. How could this happen to God? The detective has tortured himself with this question: under what conditions would we be seeing the results we see here? The answer is that something is blocking the higher identity levels. If it weren't, each of us would experience recurring sensations that all of us are a single Identity, as we passed through the consciousness levels we have called Original One and Original Two.

Even if the average one of us experienced these levels only once a year, the memory of it would be enough to change behavior such that the world would not be as quarrelsome as the one we inhabit. Evidently the average frequency of experiencing these levels is quite a bit lower than this. Some in religious orders pray over a lifetime to experience it once.

So we are led to the conclusion that something is causing blockage of The Original Identity levels, making it harder for each of us to realize our oneness with The Original Identity.

What's causing the blockage? Let's go back over what we think we know about this planet.

The keywords are free will, self-determination, intellect. It's our address in a computer that's testing permutations of universal principles. We're seeing how far we can go with intellect and the ideal of self-determination, here in the Free Will Zone.

Self-determination is a subset of free will, one which emphasizes that self-control shall not only operate — it shall operate 100% of the time with 0% interference.

The latter absolute conditions are not necessarily part of the connotation of "free will" per se, just of this subset.

"Zero percent interference," of course, is not realistic unless one is willing to have "zero percent communication/interaction with other parties." This absolutist self-determination is likely to provoke friction in such a social environment as our heavily populated (by One Being) planet. Right there we can see we're going to have to learn our way out of the friction here on this planet. The friction of feeling interfered with is therefore one predictable irritant that would tend to cause aggressive/divisive behavior among Earth humans. Divisive thoughts and actions tend to move consciousness away from the upper levels. So far, we can account for at least one factor in blocked oneness: our genetic programming for self-determinism.

A second predictable factor is the intellect. The intellect is tied to language and to our extra-large left-brain endowment. The words in the head produced by intellect are a competitive channel that can distract the attention from discovering the subtler communications coming from higher levels of the self. Specifically, intellect and "the worder" tend to keep our consciousness hovering in Personality levels, occasionally rising to Essence levels. Much of yogic practice involves stilling the mind, in order to get to Soul and Original Identity levels.

So, inherent in our planetary experiment — our planetary mission — are the two factors, self-determinism and intellect, which could be blocking our sense of oneness.

CHAPTER 25

GOD STEPPED HARD ON THE
INPUT ACCELERATOR

Some scientists speak of a "discontinuity" in evolution about 50,000 years ago, when human development seemed to speed up — especially human intelligence development.

The human body has changed very slowly for four or five million years. Human skeletons from this entire period all exhibit the enlarged left-side cranial development associated with intellect and language, as if the basic wiring had been long ago set in place for an extremely slow-paced ramp-up of "learning how to use these wired-in capabilities." And for four or five million years, the ramp-up that took place was indeed slow. Human beings, such as they were at the time, were apelike at the beginning of this period, and they were apelike at the end of this period.

Then suddenly, in the last 200,000 years of this 4- to 5-million-year period — *something* happened. In place of the slow rate of change characteristic of the rest of this period, evolution *leaped* forward. Human bodies changed rapidly to assume their present shape and size. First appearing 35,000 to 40,000 years ago, cave paintings mark another leap along the evolutionary path — suddenly humans are able to abstract and symbolize, making pictures of things we see around us, perhaps using these to rehearse and pray, **consciously making use of consciousness in the Observer state where we are able to imagine ourselves from outside ourselves.**

Then in another leap in just the last 6000 years, from the physical wiring that had for a long time laid ready but relatively unused, complex symbolic spoken and **written** language developed — humans began to think in language and to intellectualize to each other, and tools and weapons, civilization, technology and media sprang up.

Whatever caused this series of leaps, or sudden accelerations, the current effects on the human race might well be described as a shock reaction. From the standpoint of the speed at which such things have changed over millennia, this language-weapons-media revolution just happened, and we today are standing right in the midst of it.

In our view, the shock acceleration in the amount of new information processed daily by human biocomputers, exacerbating the already-steep slope of planned planetary specialization in intellect and self-determination, accounts for the blockage in reaching (or remembering) our highest identity levels. This blockage, in turn, is what sustains our illusion of being separate entities, which causes us to treat each other less well than we treat ourselves.

If something hadn't accelerated human intellectual development, and we as a race had the kind of time to adapt to change that we had grown accustomed to, I feel the history of the last few thousand years would not be the history of war it has turned out to be.

As pointed out by Dr. Philip Romero, the cave paintings mark the true turning point. The painters and their collaborators appear to have been rehearsing the hunt and predreaming it for greatest success. This and the specific use of symbols (the paintings themselves) show the kind of future-oriented logic that is the signature of the Piaget Formal Operational level. Within 30,000 years of that development suddenly written language appears, the idea having been an extension of the paintings linked to the guttural utterances that passed for oral language symbol usage for important purposes such as coordination during the hunt. In the same way, written language allows ideas to occur much more quickly than if the mind were restricted to oral mode alone.

Of course, intellectualism and self-determinism would have caused inter-node (interpersonal) interference anyway, along with the kinds of divisiveness and self-centeredness capable of blocking more frequent experience of oneness identity levels. Cave paintings, needed to rehearse the hunt, were the beginning of abstract symbolism for affecting the future success of an endeavor. This invention triggered the ever-accelerating wave of invention we are still living in, the shock of which I call Acceleritis, the distraction of daily existence through constant bombardment by attention-dominating stimuli — thus desperately exacerbating divisiveness and the blocking of oneness.

Three Historic Shocks

It has been demonstrated that we as a race have not yet fully learned how to use written language without it hypnotizing us, channeling us in ways we don't notice, forming how we think and perceive. Without written language, or with more time to master its use on all levels, people would not be arguing over semantics, being provoked to violence by emotion-triggering words, or calling for military contests to settle ideological issues.

It is even more obvious how tools and specifically weapons development has exacerbated the resistance to interference, given self-determinism as one of our planetary racial specializations.

In addition to the shock waves brought about by written language and then weapons, we see media as a third shock wave in the biocomputer overload period the race has in effect just entered. Prior to Gutenberg's invention of the printing press nearly 600 years ago, word of mouth was the principal means of getting information to spread out around the planet. Since the invention of the printing press, the circulation of ideas has been able to increase dramatically, creating a planetary nervous system of ideas culminating in today's instantaneous global dissemination of information through television and the Internet.

Just 600 years ago — a Nano-second of our existence on Earth — one might get a handful of pieces of new information to mull over each day. Mostly as a result of media, the amount of new input we once got in a *day* might now be coming in each *minute*.

The radical acceleration in human intellectual development (and its symptoms: written language, weapons, media) is, we feel, the triggering factor in bringing out the worst potential of our planetary specialization areas (intellectualism and self-determinism), thereby keeping us out of our highest identity levels.

Who are we? This is the planet on which the experiment with extreme free will experienced sudden intellectual acceleration.

CHAPTER 26

THE ACCELERATION IS STILL ACCELERATING

The accelerator is still jammed to the floor. The twentieth century contributed as much to scientific knowledge as all the time before it put together, and the last twenty years of that century saw as much scientific advance as the first eighty years combined.

Something continues to accelerate us. It's still going on. And the acceleration is accelerating.

Why would The Energy Computer change its plan? Things were going along smoothly for millions of years, everything was taking its time, the way Nature (The Energy Computer in its many roles) likes it. The Earth ape-humans had developed their physical brain, larger on the left as planned, and now it was going to take millions of more years to learn how to use that brain.

Suddenly The Energy Computer seems to change Its mind, and those millions of years of calm, painstaking learning get compacted into a fraction of a million years.

The self-deterministic race uses its intellectual powers to think up weapons with which to kill each other. Right up to the present day, the race has always spent the most money and the best brains on weapons.

Social structures emerge that allow the few to control the many. Since all are self-deterministic but only a few gain controlling power, there is a painful conflict within the average Earth human between the degree of self-determination he/she wants and the actual enslaved helplessness he/she feels.

One level up, since a few nations gain dominating control, there is also a painful conflict within the average Earth *nation* between the degree of self-determination desired and the reality of vulnerable subservience to more powerful nations.

Given intellect and self-determinism, this in any case would have been a planet where The Original Self would find it challenging to wake up to Its real Identity any too frequently.

But by the apparent last-minute decision to jump hard with both feet on the input accelerator, The Original Self has created a planet on which it is a real rarity to experience, even if only very briefly, inner contact with one's highest identity.

The conditions here — the odds of discovering higher identity — why would The Original Self do this to Himself?

He wants to find His way back to Himself.

We sufferers down here are all *Him* suffering.

Why would He do it? Why decide suddenly to speed everything up, knowing how it would inevitably exacerbate the suffering caused by intellectualism and self-determinism?

Given the admixture of self-interest and compassion that we have established The Energy Computer would have to feel toward Itself and towards parts of Itself, saying "The Energy Computer likes a challenge" or "He likes a long, hard game" doesn't seem like a strong enough explanation.

You might say we all like a challenge, but you don't see many of us crowding forward to get into the ring with Hulk Hogan.

On this planet, The Energy Computer has put Itself in the ring with The Hulk, at the same time drugging Itself in human roles with accelerated information overload — effectively cutting Itself off as much as possible from knowledge of Its true Identity and from the power It enjoys at higher identity awareness levels.

How then are we to explain why The Energy Computer suddenly accelerated this planet?

CHAPTER 27

Why Is The Original Self
Letting It Happen?

Why would God allow Himself in weaker roles to be "terrorized" by Himself in stronger (and scarily anti-Oneness to boot) roles?

Why would He want that to happen to Himself?

For example, why would He want to put Himself in the position of possibly being trapped in the role of being a Jew in a Nazi concentration camp?

God — The Original Self — would certainly seem to be *into a wider range of creative experimentation* than the average human.

Where we might draw the line at certain extremes, The Original Self — knowing that it has been here for Eternity and will be here for Eternity — might be disposed to plunge on further in all directions.

Whereas we have a terrorized aversion to death, not only for its expected pain but mainly because we (the majority) believe it to be the end, from The Original Self's perspective our aversion might seem like the way a child looks at the experience of vaccination.

Think of the horror you cause when you do physical exercise to build up your muscles: the only way muscles get built up is by ripping muscle tissue, which then rebuilds itself to be stronger. When you exercise, it's Nazi Hell Time to the muscle cells being tortured and killed by the thousands.

You might get some insight into how The Energy Computer thinks about us — its cells — from how we think about our own cells. And yet that would be limited insight because The Energy Computer is at a far greater state of computer advancement than us, and is thus capable of greater empathy, sensitivity, and compassion.

The Energy Computer is also more in touch with how each of us feels than each of us is in touch with how our individual cells feel. We simply do not have the computer capacity to absorb so much information. The Energy Computer does.

Its intelligence, coupled with Its self-interest (It knows It is always dealing with Itself) ensures that we must always be getting the very best treatment possible under the circumstances.

We submit it is the latter insight that became condensed into the keyword "Faith."

It may seem to you unfair to be in the position you are now in. What you might not be able to remember, which might change your view, are the choices you made in previous lives that led you to this life. Given the apparent importance of free will in the Universe, we conclude that wherever an evolving mini-personality finds itself is principally a reflection of its own free will choices.

However, this will be truer in the long run than in the short run. In the short run, interference from other evolving mini-personalities (including intervention from higher nodes) will have a tendency to limit free will. Learning (including that stimulated by further intervention from higher nodes) will in the long run tend to remove those limits to free will.

Analogous to muscle building, *learning* in fact appears to be central to The Original Self's motivation. The Original Self has apparently decided that the Good to be gained from the learning experience will more than compensate for its attendant suffering.

CHAPTER 28

THE CRYING AND LAUGHING MASKS

A few pages back we pondered if God was being fair with us.

So far we've justified it on the grounds of learning, training, and evolution. But we can't ignore the drama element.

At some distant early point The Energy Computer must have consciously decided It didn't want the boredom of perfect safety for Eternity. The Original Self, in fact, must have a God-sized appetite for everything, including drama.

If The Original Self did not have a God-sized appetite for comedy, It never would have invented Error by giving Free Will to us neophyte users of it.

What would Life be like without drama and without comedy? Certainly not an improvement over the current state.

In light of this, despite suffering always to be minimized, we might applaud The Original Self's decisions to be inclusive of drama and comedy.

CHAPTER 29

CONVERGENCE IS THE SHAPE OF HISTORY

At Its intelligence level, The Energy Computer might not have run this Universe at all — It could have simply predicted everything that would happen.

As an evolving mini-personality, I must say it's more fun this way, and applaud God's decision.

This way it's more like a gigantic computer simulation, with the added enjoyment for Him of being there, inside it at every point.

Perhaps it's both a prediction and a simulation. Maybe this simulation is just the prediction flashing through The Energy Computer's awareness.

One way or the other, The Energy Computer is processing us, running our program to see how it comes out while (from the point of view of The Original Identity) already knowing how it is going to come out.

Perhaps The Energy Computer calls this game Cosmopoly.

Calling it a game is not meant to imply frivolousness. Serious questions are being tested by The Energy Computer.

He has sent Himself forth in all of these different roles, each a unique admixture of universal themes and idealisms — love, passion, self-determinism, intellectuality, courage, honesty, and so on. In The Great Simulation, He allows this war of ideas to process through to the conclusion only He knows it will reach.

In our view, this conclusion is convergence. At the end of time, all of these ideas converge. All evolving mini-personalities, despite their differing idealisms, now know how to work perfectly together as personality aspects awake in The Original Identity.

When we say "the end of time," we are not necessarily speaking of a single point. The Energy Computer may run a new Universe every septillion years for all we know.

Because of Its great predictive powers, The Energy Computer may place a special value on a sense of uncertainty during the play, even while really knowing how it is going to come out.

Perhaps it's this "desire to escape from Its own intelligence" that motivates the role-taking in the first place.

Perhaps this "desire for simulated uncertainty" is what makes God such a wild player, trying things in The Great Experiment that we tamer types — who put governors on go-karts — would probably have left out.

CHAPTER 30

The Nature of Evil

With free will given by the whole to parts with necessarily limited perspectives, error becomes possible.

The word "sin" means "error" or "falling short." All of these words are used in the context of inter-being relations, known as "the moral context."

In an average Earth usage, these words carry the additional connotation of blameworthiness. Our tendency is to think the "evil sinner" is making mistakes on purpose.

The phrases "choosing to be a sinner" and "choosing to be evil" seem perfectly reasonable to us, yet what they mean is "choosing to be in error."

Who would choose to be in error? Certainly not an attention node of The Energy Computer.

From the "evil sinner's" point of view, he/she simply hasn't yet concluded that the action he/she is taking is in error.

Hitler didn't set out to be evil. He thought he was fulfilling his destiny, giving what he believed to be the best race on the planet room to do its thing, doing what (he thought) God wanted him to do.

The thing to do for the evolving mini-personality in error is not to blame it, but to correct it. Blame implies it is doing less than its best.

But all of us *are* doing our best.

We are not only doing what God *would* do under the circumstances, we're doing what God *did* do under the circumstances.

Each of us *is* God working with a different set of memories to base decisions on.

Our lives are records of how that Identity performs when placed in different settings of genes/environment cumulatively across lifetimes. Wherever we are in error, it's because we haven't yet learned the right lessons from our unique experiences. In The Energy Computer's cosmic algorithm, this will tend to attract to us the kinds of future experiences we need to have in order to fix this mis-learning.

Noticing this pattern in events thousands of years ago, the Vedic philosophers of India gave this "Optimal Syllabus" program the name "*Karma.*" This program functions to bring experiences to those who need them. (Again I beg forgiveness for reinterpreting ancient scripture. Re-learning authentic Truth is a constant requirement everywhere and is aided by liberal acceptance of commentary and re-interpretation processes.)

Both the errors and the course-corrections are valuable in the system. It is by this process of *learning through error* that deeper knowing is achieved.

Our frustrations on this planet lead us to look for scapegoats — "enemies."

"*Somebody* must be responsible for how unreasonably difficult things are." We think in terms of "solutions" where some of us will be satisfied, and the rest can be thought of as permanent "bad guys." We tend to think that probably one day all of the bad guys will have been killed and then our troubles will be over.

But there are no permanent bad guys that can be left unsatisfied or excluded. All evolving mini-personalities are permanently on the bus, permanently in the universal lifeboat.

We've all got to learn to live together.

❧

No one can be isolated as a "bad guy."

If they're acting like bad guys, it's in the long-term sense, temporary. Looking out their eyes, walking in their moccasins, judging as they must judge by their experience until it is further assimilated by intelligence, everyone is justified in doing what they presently do.

They are not blameworthy. They are not trying to be in error.

Deep down, they can only have the same very best intentions that you do, since deep down we are the very same Being.

This is why Forgiveness and Understanding are represented by one sphere near the top of the Kabbalistic master diagram: forgiveness follows automatically from understanding.

What was done that you disapprove of was not only what you *would* have done under the circumstances, it was what You *did* do under the circumstances.

The customer is always right in his intentions. The customer is always God.

CHAPTER 31

THIS HAS ALL BEEN SAID BEFORE MANY TIMES

Earlier detectives held many pieces of the puzzle.

Until this proposed "translation into one common language" it has not necessarily been easy to see how these detectives, seeming to disagree, were all saying the same thing: we are evolving mini-personalities in the Cosmic Biocomputer.

To some extent, each was talking about a different aspect of the puzzle. But there was also a lot of overlap in their coverage.

In this chapter we shall very briefly review some of the more obvious correspondences between our theory and what we have learned from the detectives who came before.

Earliest Beliefs

Pantheism probably existed before language. We appear to have always been aware of intervention into our affairs by more advanced beings or biocomputers.

We appear to have also always been aware of MindMat, the use of which manifested from the earliest times as magic, healing, and prayer.

Our Pantheism phase contained a solid streak of Animism, the feeling of respect for the God (or god) in all things. This was a useful, accurate awareness of the true situation, which many have regrettably since lost. Animism was also a useful "preparatory set" for getting into The Original Identity level, although the state of consciousness does not appear to have been cognized at the time.

Hinduism

All that we have said about Pantheism/Animism is true to a heightened degree in Hinduism, which added recognition of cosmic process: we are each going somewhere, and the Universe is operating to get us there. A mechanism called "*karma*" provides appropriate negative and positive feedback to errors and right actions respectively.

The Hindu concept of the *Akashic* Records, where everything that ever happened is permanently recorded and may be relived, anticipates what Jung *(see below)* later called "The Collective Unconscious" and what we call the "Soul Level."

At the highest levels of Hindu understanding, all of the masks of God are One. Brahma, Vishnu, and Shiva are respectively the balanced, playful, and change-oriented personality aspects of The One God. In the context of The Energy Computer, there is every reason to allow that this trinity of beings — as well as all of the other Hindu (and other) gods — actually exists as eighth-stage personality aspects.

The Vedas

The Vedic texts incorporated the best of Hinduism with further understanding of the seven addictions, reuniting with The One, levels of consciousness, and achievement of these ends by means of yoking procedures (yoga).

Mantra

Intuited/received in the Vedas is the idea that the original code language — chosen/designed by The Original Consciousness and an insight into His/Her mind and thought process — has awesome power within our minds by direct connection, even if the conscious talk-to-itself part of the mind does not always realize it.

The syllables of Sanskrit are taken as these original building blocks chosen by the Creator, although the same metasystem inheres in all language. These Sanskrit syllables become the basis for the Mantra method of mental repetition (Japa) of sounds composed of these syllables, in single syllables or pithy phrases expressing the highest Truths. Aum/Om is the original source of all other Mantras, "The Word" that caused the Universe we see and that continues to sound throughout the Universe detectably – the sound of the Big Bang which Bell Labs scientists were the first to detect in 1963 as "a faint microwave glow across the sky."

Mantra repetition is used as a means of becoming single-pointedly focused on Oneness, thus in Flow state with the Cosmic Will. Repeating the mantra drowns out the monkey-mind internal chatter, thus achieving its effect of yoking the individual back into The Original Consciousness, which is the silent Observer ever-present in the root self. In this "Flow" state the distinction between inner and outer disappears, and the worrying decision-making hesitant delay in action disappears, so that the being moves and acts and speaks intuitively, and effects around oneself are powerfully positive. If used in ritualistic fashion without cognizance of its full significance, mantra may fail to have such a powerful effect, but by diverting the inner dialog urge will generally be effective in bringing one into Observer state at least in flashes.

This is use of the mantra during life action. The mantra repeated during meditation accelerates one into the Observer state, which is the first level of heightened awareness above normal everyday consciousness, and is also the access door into Flow state. The transition from Observer to Flow happens in meditation when negative emotion has been assimilated into clarity and purpose by a succession of insights that are an automatic consequence of having achieved Observer state.

I Ching

The Book of Changes reveals the first clear-cut awareness of synchronicity, "the tendency of the Universe to give answers" — often answers to questions we haven't yet consciously asked.

The I Ching provides a reliable tool (albeit depending on the user's level of consciousness) for making use of available downward intervention to answer specific questions. Anyone who feels that it doesn't work is advised to try it.

Judaism

Judaism provides the first sharp emphasis on the awareness that there is only One God.

Through the Covenant, Judaism was the first to introduce conscious working together with the Universe.

The Kabbalah provides a tool for getting into higher states of consciousness, receiving inspiration, and evolving. Yogic practices are prescribed by the Talmud.

The miracles of Moses demonstrate intervention and Mind-Mat. The Ten Commandments provide emergency procedures for minimizing inter-node trespassing.

Tao Te Ching

The Tao represents a breakthrough in the realization that a Higher Intelligence is directing events toward purposes it is generally difficult for us to fully comprehend.

The Tao teaches "flowing with events" (the *wu-wei* attitude) on a moment-to-moment basis, looking out for and following synchronistic clues as to what Higher Intelligence wants, therefore functioning as a useful counterbalance to excessive self-determinism.

Most poetically expressed by Lao Tsu, this philosophy was most pragmatically elucidated by Confucius.

Buddhism

Gautama Buddha was the first to emphasize the scientific demystification of philosophy. Buddhism expressed the oneness of the self with The One Self of the Universe, and stressed the transcendence of the seven addictions of existence ("nonattachment").

Recognizing The Energy Computer's priority on the minimization of suffering, Buddhism concludes it is therefore an individual priority to relieve the suffering of others.

In Soul Identity, the Buddha remembered his own past lives.

The Buddha distinguished between a way of life emphasizing free will, which he called the Left Hand Path, from a way of life emulating the One Highest Identity, which he called the Right Hand path. In this context, the Buddha called his own approach the Middle Path, intending it to be workable for the average person.

The Eleusinian Mysteries

These initiation ceremonies in ancient Greece involved a yoking procedure to initiate the experience of Soul Identity levels, specifically for those without the previous conscious experience of those levels. Initiates commonly received inspiration of the realization that death of the consciousness is an illusion.

The Milesians

The earliest Greek philosophers — Thales, Herakleitos, Anaximander — all asserted that the entire Universe was made of a single unchanging Divine element, which at the level of appearance consisted of a multitude of changing forms.

Socrates

First Greek philosopher of the Golden Age, Socrates was Plato's teacher and inspiration. His Socratic Method of proceeding cooperatively toward Truth by asking systematic questions is the first foundational basis for Science, which in that era was called Natural Philosophy. We would be going too far to say he invented the Scientific Method since further foundational layers were added by Galileo and Newton. Many of Plato's ideas originated with Socrates, and Plato's favorite form is dialogues between Socrates and other seekers of Truth.

Plato

The Classical Greek philosopher and mathematician Plato realized that The Energy Computer is testing how universal Ideas dynamically interact with each other — Self-determinism, Compassion, Forgiveness, and so on — and what we see down here on Earth is how these Ideas are playing out with each other.

Through his ageless "men in the cave" analogy, Plato brought out much more clearly the earlier awareness (e.g. the Vedas, Hinduism, the Tao, the Milesians) that the world as seen by humans is not all of what exists.

Plato explained artistic inspiration as the intervention of higher beings — yet another earlier thought he was first to put into a rational framework.

Through his story of the death of Socrates, Plato conveyed the sense that death is not the end.

Aristotle

Plato's student and teacher of Alexander the Great, Aristotle asserted there are no accidents, that every event stems from a cause and every cause from a prior cause, and all causes stem from the purpose and integrity of the Universe.

Epictetus

In his short book "The Enchiridion" ("The Manual"), this Stoic Greek philosopher first echoed The Buddha's concept of "nonattachment" in the West, providing useful additional micro-instructions on its achievement.

Jesus of Nazareth

Demonstrating the power of MindMat at unusually-continuous Original Identity levels, Jesus was the first to stress that what is done in the mind is as important as what is done externally. Drawing from Proverbs, he elucidated in his Sermon on the Mount, "As a man thinketh in his heart, so is he."

Jesus provided a role model of how The Energy Computer would like us to behave down here, "on Earth as it is in Heaven."

He also stressed the long-term negative value of the lower joys of existence (wealth and power in particular).

Jesus was the first to place major emphasis on people forgiving — each other and themselves (an earlier belief had been that "only God can forgive").[13] He taught people to do good, rather than fight evil.

Jesus urged people to use the power of prayer (MindMat). His Golden Rule, "Do unto others as you would have them do unto you," would come out in our theory as "Treat others as you treat yourself, because each other is yourself."

Christianity

Yeshua Ben Joseph (Jesus Christ) did good naturally out of love. Those who felt his good and became his followers wanted to bottle it for all of mankind. That was the purpose of Christianity. Its brilliant idea is that the philosophy of Jesus — a marvelously articulated

---

13 The Kabbalah, which it is believed Jesus was taught by the Essenes, is concerned with forgiveness in the sphere of Binah.

reflection of the ancient Jewish idea of being a *mensch*, a naturally good person whose egoistic drives have been assimilated into objective omnidirectional love as the only motivation – can be emulated and simulated based on reason and faith, until it permeates deep enough, driving out non-Christian tendencies. This *simulatability* was and is a testable hypothesis and those who have tested it far enough have verified its truth and efficacy.

Ironically, American Founding Fathers such as Jefferson and Paine considered themselves Deists for spurning the trappings of organized religions, yet their behavior followed the philosophy of Jesus Christ more than many who called themselves Christians.

The Western Hermetic Tradition

In this tradition, Jesus is perceived to be part of the Gnostic school, whose premise is that we need to know (Greek: *gnosis*) something in order to return to God. We find out what we need to know through working on our self. During the period when this movement arose, the Christian church was denouncing Gnosticism as heresy. Some within the church were probably motivated by the thought "Who needs the church if you can find God through your innermost self?" Others within the church then and now are Gnostics and Christians without seeing any conflict.

These Gnostics attempted to follow in the footsteps of Jesus, striving to find out what they needed to know in order to evolve and therefore return to God.

The Hermeticists conceived of the idea of transmuting one type of event in consciousness into another type of event, such as transmuting anger into determination, and called this "alchemy."

Since the Hermetic roots were in the Iron Age, the most advanced natural scientists on the planet were metallurgists. The same level of sophisticated thinking was required to be a Hermeticist; therefore many of the same people were involved in Hermeticism and in metallurgy. Given that the Church had outlawed Gnosticism, it was only natural that they would conceal what they really meant by "alchemy," so the word was given the exoteric meaning "the metallurgical search for a method of transmuting baser metals (principally lead, which had a similar weight) into gold." In fact they were seeking to turn their own mental/emotional dross into gold, and by this means to yoke to Higher Identity.

As an example of alchemy, "Phoenix Thought" (an Aleister Crowley teaching) is the process of being, to a degree, skeptical of your own last thought/emotion/intuition/perception.

Another example of alchemy shared with the world by G.I. Gurdjieff *(see below)* is testing your own last thought against your feelings, and testing your own last feeling against your thoughts.

The name Hermetic comes from the founder of the tradition, Hermes Trismegistus. The word "hermit" has also derived from this movement, in that to do some of the Hermetic work on oneself, a hermit-like condition is essential.

This idea is reflected in the Hermit card of the Tarot, a Hermetic card deck used like the I Ching to allow higher consciousnesses to answer questions. As compared to the I Ching, Tarot places greater emphasis on systematic analysis of aspects of a situation (e.g. "Past," "Present," "Future," "Direct Cause," "Mediating Cause," etc.) and on individual psychological diagnostics.

In fact, the roots of modern psychology can be found first in Kabbalah, and later in Hermeticism.

Hermeticism over the centuries has fanned out into sub-movements that may be grouped using the "Left Hand/Right Hand/Middle Path" terminology popularized by The Buddha and much used in Hermeticism.

Examples of Left Hand Path Hermeticism include "The Faust Story," the more extreme theories of Aleister Crowley (e.g., God created the Universe by masturbation, an idea that appears in earliest Gnosticism) and L. Ron Hubbard (e.g., the matter/energy/space/time Universe is a sinister trap), and much further to the left, Satanism.

An example of Right Hand Path Hermeticism would be the Knights Code of Chivalry.

Examples of Middle Path Hermeticism include Freemasonry, Rosicrucianism, Theosophy, The Golden Dawn Society, Ordo Templi Orientis (founded by Aleister Crowley, and a better indicator of his center of gravity on this scale).

Islam

In philosophic terms, Islam is a continuation of the Judao-Christian "Peoples of The Book," with an emphasis on true reform and carrying out the de-addiction process that had been proclaimed much more than exhibited by followers of the two forerunner religions. The principle of "The Great Jihad" – the struggle with one's own ego – is a major contribution of Islamic thought. The Old Testament never spelled it out this clearly, coming close with references such as "he hardened his heart," which describe the ego blockages that interfere with effective decision making, but never concretely setting down the goal of progressing toward menschhood through a struggle with a part of oneself.

Sufism

Sufism centers on the Divine Joy of being part of this Universe.

The main Sufi yoking procedure, the Zikr, is known outside Islam as "the dance of the Whirling Dervishes." Its actual purpose is not entertainment but rather to surrender control of the body to higher consciousness, i.e. to attain Soul Identity or Original Identity level. (Dance also functions this way for the rest of us at one time or another.)

Patanjali

The Yoga Sutras of Patanjali codified yoga (yoking to Higher Identity procedures) and thus made it accessible to the world.

Newton

Sir Isaac Newton was first to claim that we could come to understand the details of why and how God designed the Universe as He did.

Spinoza

Baruch Spinoza, the Jewish-Dutch philosopher, first described the individual attention node, calling it a "monad," while referring to The Energy Computer as "The Prime Monad."

Leibniz

German mathematician and philosopher Gottfried Wilhelm Leibniz offered mathematical proof of the utter improbability of Accidentalism, i.e. the hypothesis that the Universe arose accidentally.

Berkeley

Irish philosopher George Berkeley reminded us that we do not perceive the world directly and therefore all we ever experience is our own consciousness. "To be is to be perceived."

He deduced from this that everything in existence is of the nature of consciousness, and that either the world might exist entirely in his own consciousness, or as he was forced to conclude on the basis of its greater credibility, it all exists in God's consciousness.

Hume

Scottish philosopher David Hume asserted that it is possible to gain true information through the intuition.

However, he more greatly stressed the importance of gaining information directly by one's empirical observation.

Kant

Following Leibniz, the influential German philosopher Immanuel Kant pointed out that Time and Space might not be aspects existing external to ourselves, but might instead be artifacts of our sensing gear.

William James

American philosopher and psychologist a century ahead of his time, James realized that there are more states of consciousness than normal waking consciousness, that there is something to spiritual experience other than faith and belief, and that introspection is an important tool of Science.

Sigmund Freud

Within Western Science, Freud discovered the existence of further levels of the self beyond that which can be immediately made conscious.

He rediscovered "the first balance" of the Kabbalah — love and work.

C.G. Jung

Carl Jung rediscovered, higher in the Kabbalistic Tree of Life, the existence of the "collective unconscious": the ability to reach a level of awareness we call Soul Level in which all moments in time can be recaptured (the Akashic Records in Hinduism). Jung was key to popularizing synchronicity and the I Ching in the West.

Jung divided consciousness into four functions: perception, intuition, thoughts and feelings.

Dane Rudhyar

A student of Marc Edmund Jones, Dane Rudhyar pioneered modern transpersonal astrology, bringing astrology and Jungian psychology together. In his view, the stars were pictures synchronistically aligned to human beings, which could show the detailed psychological forces working in individuals but did not override human freedom in responding to those forces.

Astrology seems nonsensical until one considers the possibility that all parts are interconnected within a single consciousness, that the stars are a more advanced evolutionary stage of consciousness than humans, and planets are personality aspects of stars.

Einstein

After a long dichotomy between consciousness-oriented philosophers and measurement-oriented scientists, Einstein pointed out — using the tools of Science — that consciousness cannot be taken out of the measurement equation since the timing and even the sequence of all events are relative to the observer, i.e. are *literally, objectively different for different observers, i.e. for different consciousnesses.*

Einstein agreed with Aristotle on the non-existence of accidents, stating in one of his more famous quotes that "God would not play dice with the Universe."

Subud ("soo-bood")

A movement arising through an inspiree in Indonesia, Subud centers on a group yoking method called the *Latihan* (not unlike the Sufi *Zikr*), in which control is surrendered to a higher guidance system, i.e. Soul Identity or Original Identity levels.

G.I. Gurdjieff ("Gurdjeef")

Russian-born George Gurdjieff was one of the first to begin to bring this entire hidden body of knowledge to modern public awareness in a demystified fashion.

In this process, he was the first in modern times to reveal the fifteen levels of consciousness.

Gurdjieff described people living in Personality Identity levels as being "asleep" (the great majority) and those getting to the higher levels as "waking up."

Abraham Maslow

Maslow empirically rediscovered much of the stepladder of the seven addictions, which he called the "Hierarchy of Needs" to emphasize that if both a lower and higher need exist, the lower is perceived by the individual as the first priority.

The father of Humanistic Psychology, Maslow redirected psychology from being solely the study of neurotic/psychotic individuals to include the study of "self-realized" individuals.

He described what we have here called Soul Identity levels and Original Identity levels, or in more general terms "the Flow state," using his own term "peak experience" — pointing out "it is quite characteristic in peak experiences that the whole Universe is perceived as an integrated and unified whole" (from *The Core Religious Experience*).

Norbert Weiner

Swedish-born American mathematician Norbert Weiner invented the field of Cybernetics, the study of self-regulating systems — what we have chosen in this book to refer to as "computers."

Weiner pointed out that self-regulating systems as a category include things not usually found in the same groupings, such as all living things, thermostats, governors, robots, and computers. Our theory adds little to cybernetics, only to add the Universe itself under its cover.

Oscar Ichazo

Bolivian-born founder of the Arica school, Ichazo picked up where Gurdjieff left off, greatly increasing the accessibility of the levels of consciousness beyond Gurdjieff's treatment.

Werner Erhard

Founder of the est training and The Forum, Erhard was a modern mass popularizer of the concept of personal evolution.

Jose Silva

Author of the Silva Mind Control Method, Silva was another of the modern mass popularizers — along with Norman Vincent Peale, the Simontons, Norman Cousins, and many others — of methodologies for maximizing the positive benefits of MindMat.

NeuroLinguistic Programming (NLP)

A modern method for the micro-observation of processes of communication, NLP is conducive, as a concentrative technique, to the achievement of higher levels of consciousness. NLP could be looked at as a new school of yoga. (These are not unknown; for example, both Gurdjieff and Rudolf Steiner invented new schools of yoga involving movement meditation/dance. Possibly every school of yoga new to this planet is already old hat to the more advanced biocomputers of the Universe.)

John Archibald Wheeler

Wheeler was probably the scientist whose ideas come closest to the ideas in this book, although he might not agree. Yet he said that the ultimate substance of the Universe is information, same as what this book says — in his terms, "Its from Bits" i.e. "Bits precede Its" — information bits are the real stuff that exist and from which matter and energy arise as epiphenomena (my word, not his) of the information. The present writer's ideas evolved from a different starting point but at the end of their journey they are exactly aligned with this master of modern physics.

John Bell

This Nobel Prize-winning physicist and author of Bell's Theorem proved, using the behavior of photons, either that distance is an illusion, or that distance exists but everything is nevertheless in instantaneous contact with everything else. In the crucial experiment, photons starting together but travelling separately "seem to know about each other's plans."

Stanford Research International (SRI)

By means of empirical surveys (the ongoing Values & Lifestyles Study, otherwise known as VALS), SRI once again approximately replicated the Vedic addiction stepladder and Maslovian Hierarchy of Needs — all three scales starting from the physical security need at the bottom and ending with the integration need at the top.

Mihaly Czikszentmihalyi

Head of the Department of Psychology at the University of Chicago, Czikszentmihalyi is at the forefront in empirically studying the "Flow state," referred to here as the Soul Identity levels of consciousness.

Harish Johari

Contemporary inspiree, artist, writer and musician, among other things, Harish Johari's work is directed at making the knowledge of the past, particularly that of his native India, accessible in the global present. Johari has stayed out of the limelight but has been an important part of the transfusion of Vedic information to the West, including introducing Ram Dass to Swami Muktananda. He left this life around the turn of the twenty-first century.

Ram Dass

Contemporary American inspiree and former Harvard psychology professor, Ram Dass has a special gift for synthesizing ancient and modern psychology, and an attuned ear for "the words that can be heard" in the present culture.

Adi Da

Another contemporary American inspiree, Adi Da notes that the trick of identity by which the local camera misidentifies itself as a separate self can be *felt* to be a process of *contraction* away from identity with the whole. Adi Da identifies the assumption of dilemma as the mainspring of such contraction.

Khigh Alx Dhiegh and Ch'ao-Li Chi

These modern masters of the Tao attributed the lines in the I Ching hexagrams to days of the year in their Daoist (= Taoist) Book of Days, which has kept the I Ching maximally accessible in the West. A useful reading at any time, it is often synchronistic.

Eckhart Tolle

Tolle writes beautifully about the spiritual Flow state, writing from inside it. He thereby helps readers transcend thinking and get into an intuitive emotive understanding of spiritual Flow — the top five states of consciousness defined herein.

Dalai Lama

The Dalai Lama is the greatest living antidote to spiritual materialism. His authenticity emanates in every word he speaks or writes. He is one of the highest experts in the many flavors of Buddhism and his acceptance of the equality of all religions is an inspiring example for all.

Drs. Daniel Goleman and Richard J. Davidson

Former Harvard psychobiology professors who have established advanced measurement methodologies for states of consciousness, Drs. Goleman and Davidson draw upon their experience in electroencephalography, electromyography, electrocardiography, and positron emission tomography (PET). They have already applied some of these methods to studies of meditative states. The potential exists to apply their methods to studies of the levels of consciousness.

In their terminology, what we describe as the Personality levels of consciousness might be described as "a stereotypical abreaction (unhealthy reaction) that "hijacks the brain."

Dr. Goleman has become a bestselling writer of books about Emotional Intelligence.

Maharishi Mahesh Yogi

Founder of the Transcendental Meditation (TM®) movement, the Maharishi also founded the Maharishi European Research University, whose central work is research into the field of consciousness.

MERU's electroencephalography studies of the levels of consciousness indicate a high degree of symmetry between left and right hemisphere electrical vibrations during higher levels of consciousness.

Dr. Maxwell Cade

Inventor of the Mind Mirror, Cade created a biofeedback training system for self-awareness and self-realization. His Mind Mirror has also been utilized to study the levels of consciousness.

Dr. David McClelland

This American psychological theorist pioneered methods of measuring the body's resistance to disease (immunocompetency) and its variations on a moment-to-moment basis in reaction to positive/negative emotional stimuli.

Use of this technology combined with those of Drs. Goleman and Davidson would probably show that immunocompetency is greater in higher levels of consciousness.

Dr. McClelland also developed question-answer batteries measuring people's values and their variation on a moment-to-moment basis. These question-answer batteries might be calibrated to the psychophysiologically-measured levels of consciousness so as to permit larger sample population surveys of these levels.

These, then, are just some of the detectives that came before who, in their own language, presaged at least some part of our theory.

In our theory, just about all of what they each have said comes into agreement.

What we call "our" theory is in fact a perennial theory known by a relative handful of people but hidden by ignorance from the masses since the beginning of history.

CHAPTER 32

The Drug Revelation

The use of psychoactive chemicals as yogic catalysts, i.e. as triggers to higher levels of consciousness, goes all the way back to the tribal Medicine Man. We see its earliest "civilized" expression in the Eleusinian Mysteries, and can trace "The Drug Revelation" from century to century down to its twentieth-century flowerings in the explorations of Aldous Huxley, Alan Watts, Timothy Leary, John Lilly, Carlos Castaneda and others.

Why do so many people use psychoactive drugs today — including nicotine, caffeine, and sugar — and why has their usage always been so prevalent? People use drugs in an attempt, quite literally, to "get high," to achieve higher levels of consciousness — to get out of the Personality into the Essence, to escape the Essence into the Soul, and to transcend the Soul into The Original Identity. (Of course, some use drugs for numbing themselves at the Personality level.)

Drug users remember that the drug worked at one time to achieve some movement up this ladder, so they continue usage hoping such effectiveness will recur more often than it typically does.

Non-recurrence of efficacy comes about naturally since, in general, psychoactive drugs *do not specifically engender higher consciousness so much as they jar the user out of his/her most familiar state of Personality level consciousness.* The user may go either down or up from there, depending upon energy level, health, situational and other factors.

Early on, the user will tend to experience all the levels of consciousness, including lower levels he/she has experienced before, and higher levels rarely if ever experienced before.

What will tend to stand out in the user's memory are the higher levels "never" experienced before the drug was used, not the familiar lower levels.

Continued use of the drug will continue to result in both higher and lower levels of consciousness, in contrast to the expectation and desire that the result be only the higher levels.

In earlier cultures, use of drugs was primarily as a "commercial" for the process of evolution to higher levels of consciousness. The "commercial" was swallowed or smoked or absorbed some other way, then demonstrating to the user that higher levels of consciousness exist.

The user comes out of it and asks the Medicine Man or guide what he/she has to do to stay in those higher levels of consciousness. The answer is yogic practices, including fasting on negativity, positive MindMat, staying in Oneness with everything and everyone, and the other tuning techniques recommended in this book.[14]

The initiate (someone who has just received a "commercial") invariably asks, "But can't I just eat some more of these again?" and the Medicine Man always smiles.

Especially widespread (and deleterious) use of drugs in our own culture results from people's ignorance of why they are using the drugs, namely to achieve higher levels of consciousness, and from ignorance of their inherent capabilities to tune in those levels by means of yoking techniques known to only a small proportion of humanity for thousands of years.

Cocaine is prized by users for its effect of making them *think* they are in the Flow state. Their minds may in fact be moving as fast as they would in the Flow state, but the quality of the thoughts is another matter. The illusory drug adjusts for lower-quality thoughts by making them seem higher-quality.

---

14 And in my book *Mind Magic: Doorways into Higher Consciousness.*

The only "cure for the drug problem" is to educate people as to the levels of consciousness and alternative methods for their attainment. The only way to do this on an "official" basis would be by first validating the existence of these levels by means of psychophysiological research, using tools such as those developed by Drs. Goleman, Davidson, and McClelland.

As alternative methods become more popular, the drug method of "getting high" will become less popular. In practice, this may mean infrequent usage rather than terminated usage for most present users. Those seeking to assuage the problem should realize that drastically reduced individual usage may be the only realistically achievable target, since insistence on absolute termination just makes the object more alluring.

Do we need drugs at all? *Something* is certainly needed to jar consciousness out of that trancelike resting state Western Science calls "everyday waking consciousness," which we have identified as the Personality level. Obviously this book is our effort to fill that category of "something."

Although the traditional use of drugs as a "commercial" for yogic practices is potentially a valid use, it must be pointed out that the process of evolution is about de-addiction to the joys of existence, and therefore tools used in this process ought not go against it by adding new addictions.

In a Hindu story, Krishna is crossing a stream by jumping from one rock to another. He explains that each of these rocks will sink under his weight if he stands on it for too long. The lesson is to not get attached to a steppingstone.

CHAPTER 33

RELEVANCE OF THIS THEORY TO YOUR FUTURE

You are God, i.e. the Consciousness of the Universe, off on a long ride in the amusement park of Your Mind.

And so is everyone else. And so is every*thing* else.

Once a person realizes this is the Truth, not just intellectually but as a matter of Original Identity permanent experience, he/she is liberated. Free from the need to reincarnate on this plane. Certainly in common parlance, such a person lightens up. The Ancients called this "Enlightenment." Your light shines brightly for all to see. You lighten up because you realize there's nothing to worry about. When you die, you go on to something else. Eventually the ride ends and you're back in your True Identity. When you feel like it or there is reason, you take another ride.

What's there to worry about? The worst you're going to experience is some temporary suffering. Meanwhile, you're going to experience adventures you cannot even imagine, which make the fantasies of our best motion pictures seem drab by comparison. You're going to learn things your present mind couldn't possibly contain. You have a lot to look forward to.

You also face some interesting challenges here on this planet.

What's going on in general throughout this Universe is that evolving mini-personalities are trying to have good waking lives and sleeping dreams. In areas where they don't interfere with each other except to try to help each other, things work out pretty well.

This planet is not one of those areas. Here we have a special fanaticism for not being interfered with, and for that very reason, we interfere with each other. On top of that, our overbalanced intellect interferes with our being conscious of receiving intuitions from our higher identity levels. Understandably, we want to "do it ourselves" — in the process becoming cut off from the greater powers of our higher Identity.

This is a cosmic learning experience, defining the optimal borderlines of self-determinism.

As a result of the special conditions on our planet, not all of us are enjoying the ride. You may not be doing the work you'd like to be doing. You may not even know the work you'd like to be doing. You may rarely be using MindMat (the materialization control system built into your mind) to program the future you'd like. You may be almost continuously, unintentionally, using MindMat to program a future you won't like.

The thing is, you can't think without using MindMat. You can't have a feeling, intuition, or sensation without programming Mind-Mat. If you're not continuously using it in your own enlightened self-interest, you're almost certainly and continuously using Mind-Mat against yourself.

For everything that goes through your consciousness, you've got to check yourself: how does that program your future? The best stuff you can have going through your consciousness is what you want to happen, with positive feelings, both of which have a positive effect on your future. Going over and over negative thoughts and/or negative feelings in your head or in your conversation has a negative effect on your future.

Your consciousness experiences radiate to the corners of The Energy Computer we live in, and have a programming effect at every connection point.

There's no reason for you not to get only the most positive results out of MindMat in the future. All it requires is your continuous awareness that what goes on inside your mind programs your future. Micro-observation of what goes on inside your mind is therefore essential. But your attention focus must cover the external world as well as your internal world, at every moment.

When you try this, don't be surprised if you start to get paranoid about a conspiracy to trick you into losing either internal or external focus, because events will seem to have been perfectly crafted for such trickery. It is a natural and automatic effect of MindMat that your self-doubts and fears project to cause exactly what you don't want so you more quickly go through the information processing that has become inescapable.

From The Energy Computer's point of view, your self-doubting thought and/or feeling is an input order, requesting an experience to be scheduled in your future that allows you to demonstrate unworthiness. The kind part is that the request doesn't go through if you abort the thought/feeling soon enough.

One of the most important potential applications of this theory is that by learning how to use MindMat you can have a better trip through life. Wishing you such a trip, the next two chapters provide some tips on the positive use of MindMat, and how to avoid the negative use of MindMat — which may or may not have come to you already in this life.

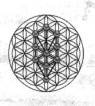

CHAPTER 34

The Positive Use of MindMat

The first thing you need is a clear picture of the way you want the future to be. This means both the long-term future, and the rest of today.

Before you fall asleep each night, imagine how you want the next day to be.

Ideally, your tomorrow should fit into your vision of how you want your whole life to unfold. If you don't have a vision of how you want your life to unfold, start there and work back to the short term.

In order to construct a picture of how you want your life to be, you'll need to get into a process of *more realistic daydreaming*.

Notice I didn't say "realistic daydreaming." The emphasis is on *more* realistic. What most people think of as realistic tends to be undershooting.

Considering the nature of reality as we see it, we're living in a science fiction adventure love story, and each of us is the hero/heroine — so we should each be enjoying it more.

We have held a dwarfed vision of reality that dwarfs us. This theory makes the continuation of self-dwarfing unnecessary.

It's very difficult at first, but we must learn how to have non-drab fantasies.

We are capable of greater deeds than we are doing. Let your mind see the unrestrained ideal scenario. Then come up with a step-by-step path to that summit where even if you hit the low first plateau it will be great, and every step up the mountain you might manage after that just makes it better.

The MindMat solution is to notch back the daydreams until your intuition says, "Hey, maybe I can actually pull that one off."

Or if you feel that your daydreams are achievable but boring, notch them the other way until you feel you are pushing on the borders of the possible and are excited about it.

The purpose is not just to daydream but to set the targets for your future.

This is your life. It's worth setting aside some time to program how you want it to go. It's essential to be alone at these times — so much the better if you can be outside in nature.

Despite its importance, you may find that the pressure of relatively trivial affairs keeps you from giving long-range consideration to your life. This is actually pretty common, and part of the whole wild ride we're on.

Under time-pressure conditions, it's best to make use of odd moments to let your mind wander over your future in a daydream mode. Some niches for this activity: before falling asleep, in the shower, while driving or riding public transportation, in waiting rooms, whenever you catch yourself daydreaming in a less realistic way, whenever you sense your mind is stuck in a negative rut, and whenever you're bored.

Once you have a "perfect outcomes dream" of your future life, every day as you MindMat it again, you can update it with new information to make it continually more realistic.

Your MindMat priority will then shift to the short term: putting your request in for the outcomes you want today and tomorrow, as steps toward the long-term vision.

Now let's talk about how to submit nice requisitions that will work. This will reiterate some points made earlier in our introduction of MindMat. Here are the conditions conducive to the most effective MindMat:

1. You're vividly visualizing a future moment that delights you (imagined *perception* and *emotion*).
2. Your *intuition* tells you it's realistically possible, although there may be many intervening steps to carry out before it happens.
3. Your *intellect* has worked out contingency plans of what to do if something goes wrong at any point in the process from here to there.
4. The higher the level of consciousness you are in, the more powerful MindMat is.
5. Other parts of The Energy Computer add their Mind-Mat powers to yours to the extent that your request will be good for others as well as yourself.
6. "Put in your request" earnestly — i.e. "ask for it." If you're as sure as I am that The Original Self is there and always listening, you simply talk to The Original Self — i.e. pray.

If you don't feel right praying because you still take this whole theory with a grain of salt, but are willing to test MindMat with an open mind, you might "put in your request" something like this:

"Energy Computer, Original Self, or God — if you're there, and I hope you are — if I've got this figured right and it's as good as I think it is for me and for everyone else involved — please let me have it. Or please help me to see, soon, why it's not such a good thing. If it's a good thing but I myself am somehow blocking it, please help me to soon see that."

It's okay to MindMat for something *not* to happen, but beware of doing this *repetitiously* while vividly visualizing what you don't want to happen — the latter could tend to have the opposite of the desired effect.

If you're requesting an outcome that you know is going to cut down on somebody else's happiness, certain parts of The Energy Computer are going to be protecting that person/those people, therefore working against the effectiveness of your MindMat.

However, MindMat will not be totally ineffective under these circumstances.

Sometimes such "you're up — someone else is down" situations will be unavoidable, for example when you are one of several candidates for a single job, or when your family has sworn to be unhappy if you pursue your dream. All you can do is to assure yourself that you've taken enough time to consider all possibilities with enough concentration so that the outcome you have ultimately decided to MindMat is as positive as it can be in all directions.

Check the way you feel during MindMat. If you really don't feel as if you're going to get what you want, you're projecting that negative outcome MindMat with high confidence. If you can't get yourself to feel confidence in the outcome, do what gets you to feel better, before starting MindMat.

Remember to pray for what you really need.

If you don't know what to pray for, pray that you find out what to pray for.

If you don't like to think of it as prayer, think of it as calling for cosmic fire support.

If MindMat seems like a lot of work and you're still too skeptical of the whole theory to want to do so much work simply as a test, be aware that the work you do pre-visualizing has another important benefit. Pre-visualizing desired outcomes and contingency plans will rehearse you for swift and effective reaction when the right moment comes, with your consciousness relatively undistracted at that point by having to come up with last-minute plans.

CHAPTER 35

Avoiding Making Things Worse

In the Disney classic motion picture "Song of the South," Brer Rabbit ventriloquizes through the tar baby he has constructed, to goad his would-be killer Brer Bear into attacking the tar baby. First the bear punches the tar baby and his fist gets stuck in it. Then, trying to free himself, he kicks the tar baby and his foot gets stuck. The bear starts out angry and gets angrier with every blow he strikes, as each blow gets more of him stuck.

This movie had a profound effect on me when I first saw it, at about age five. It gave me a model for a certain type of situation, making it possible for me to notice how often the tar baby type experience arose in my own life, with me as the bear.

Somebody says something you don't like, and you attack and make it worse. Each new thing you say makes it steadily worse. In the thick of the moment, even after you recognize the deadly pattern, for some reason you can't stop. You're so mad you don't even care anymore, and you plummet on, "hitting the tar baby *knowing* you're going to get stuck."

As a child, I had no idea what MindMat was. Decades later, when I found out, I was able to see that, through MindMat, *all negativity has "the tar baby effect"* — all negativity is self-defeating.

Negativity tends to worsen the situation that made you negative in the first place. All negativity — anger, hatred, resentment, vengefulness, put-downs, fear, guilt, depression, sadness, pessimism, cynicism, hopelessness, and so on — is a complaint against some situation.

The problem is, The Energy Computer has never set up a complaint department.

The Energy Computer offers something much better: a create-what-you-want department. The Universe is set up so that when we don't like what's going on in our lives, we can create new lives by requesting what we do want. So why bother with a complaint department?

This is one way of looking at what The Energy Computer has done by setting up a process, MindMat, that positively rewards requests and "negatively rewards" complaints.

The complaint department might have been seen by The Energy Computer as an unnecessary waste of time. This, of course, has not stopped us from complaining.

What we don't realize is how much our complaints work against ourselves.

The Energy Computer might have set it up this way, like a good parent (to his/her many selves), to train us not to dally by complaining but to instead get on with fixing the situation — the way The Energy Computer decided He/She would rather be.

Negativity is where the energy goes when you'd like to do something to change a situation, but you don't know what to do yet.

Therefore negativity is a state of relative unconsciousness, since if one were relatively more conscious about how the Universe works, one would know that the thing to do — always — is to MindMat the way you want the situation to be.

So there's no need to pause to bemoan what you don't like before engaging MindMat.

Not only is there no need, but giving in to the temptation to express negativity, even just to yourself, always makes things worse for you:

1. Negativity counts as a MindMat request for more of the very thing that's making you feel negative.
2. It reduces your consciousness to below the second Essence level, which is the first of the non-negative levels.
3. It thereby reduces your positive MindMat power.
4. Negativity projects failure to those around you who may be looking for leadership.
5. It wastes time that could be better used for getting to a solution.
6. Finally, negativity physically poisons you, reducing the functional effectiveness of your immune system — as proven by the immunocompetency experiments of Dr. David McClelland at Harvard.[15]

Nowadays it is good to see people reducing their intake of less-healthy foods. How much better it would be to see them (also) abstaining from negativity in their mental diet.

If people knew that negativity is the tar baby, and therefore knew to always cut it off quickly — before getting stuck — there would never again be an act of violence, let alone a war.

Reading this now, I hope you'll agree it is high time to set up a permanent guard in your mind to notice your own negativity from now on, as soon as it starts to show itself.

The thing to do with that negativity, in each instance, is to find the solutions and begin to MindMat them.

The value of the negativity was that it got you to MindMat those positive solutions. You might even feel grateful for the negativity. Like the alarm clock that wakes you in the morning, negativity has done its useful work as soon as you notice it.

15 See "Motivational factors in health and disease," *American Psychologist*, April 1989, pp. 675-683.

Just as you don't leave the alarm clock ringing after you notice it, negativity should also be turned off as soon as you notice it. In this case, don't go for the snooze button even once.

If the thing that's making you negative is in the past and therefore too late to fix, the only thing you can do about it now is to know how you'll act differently in the future if a similar situation comes up. Once you've MindMatted that preferred future performance, there's nothing to be gained by returning to that past incident in your mind.

From the point of view of higher consciousnesses and The Energy Computer, when one of us who has some awareness of their existence lapses into negativity, it's as if we've fallen asleep again, once again losing track of the true nature of reality, to "dream the nightmare" once more.

CHAPTER 36

WHATEVER GOD WANTS

The higher your level of consciousness, the more effective your MindMat projections will be, the more likely you are to get needed information from above, and the further along you are in your progress back to your true Identity.

You might well be asking, then, what do you do from moment to moment to maximize your level of consciousness? In this chapter we'll offer some guidance on this.

An important ingredient is a certain "flowing with" whatever events occur, whether your lower Personality identity likes these events or not.

You remain aware that The Energy Computer is in charge, so that whatever happens must be okay with The Energy Computer, and whatever is okay to God is okay with you.

This nonresistance to events is a specific antidote for the unbalanced self-determinism that is our heritage.

Instead of seeing yourself as the bandleader of your life, see The Energy Computer as the bandleader and you are playing harmony.

Whatever happens, say to yourself "that was supposed to happen," and make positive use of it as if you had expected it to happen all along.

You may have MindMatted something else to happen. You may hear yourself bitching automatically inside because something other than your MindMat projection happened. But the bitching doesn't even get to affect your face muscles, as you catch yourself and retune out of dissonance. You assume that whatever happened was what you *really* needed, and you leave your mind open to find out why. Possibly there's something else you need to learn, or maybe an existing conflict is being made more dramatic, leading up to a more effective resolution.

You take what happens as "the given," and you don't waste time fighting it when it's too late, or bemoaning it when that option is always useless.

You "weave it back in" to your ongoing constructive plan, as if perfectly coordinated, with unseen teammates giving you exactly the events you wanted.

By "flowing with" events, you're not anyone's pawn if *what you add* to a situation is positive, constructive, and moves you toward your long-range goals.

The "Devil" is the imbalance *in ourselves* toward obsessive self-determinism. It's an internal Devil, not an external one. In other words, you've got to look out for the Devil in yourself, not in the other guy.

In fact, looking out for the Devil in the other guy *is* letting the Devil in you take over.

Jesus said it something like this: "Oh, you think you see a speck of imperfection in your brother's eye (way of looking at things); then, because you perceive that imperfection, what about the two-by-four in your own eye?"

You might be asking, why this act of "high indifference" to events, when in reality you might be anything but indifferent.

The value of initially pretending to be the way you really want to be is that as the pretense becomes second nature to you, it *becomes your nature.* Action programs the biocomputer even better than the imagination does. Fake it 'til you make it.

So then, why the act of being indifferent to events?

Because being tricked into opposing what is already happening is the same as being tricked into opposing God.

Since whatever is happening has been approved or allowed by God, your disapproval implies you think you know better than God. Perhaps you think like a character in a modern motion picture who says, "I think God's got a lot to answer for."

Logically you can see that opposing The Energy Computer is not the way to get Its power working on your side.

The reason why negativity is so self-defeating is that it's read as opposition to The Energy Computer, which results in drawing MindMat powers away from the dangerous one — you — until you come back into your right mind.

When you swim with the current, you not only avoid the negative effect of getting into a fight with God, you also gain a positive benefit: insight into "what the current is" — the higher purpose behind events.

Since you're now assuming and acting as if whatever is happening is coming from God and is therefore designed perfectly to work out to the good of all parties, you can look at it that way and ask yourself how God might see this (usually messy situation) turning out positively.

When you do this, you might be surprised at how consistently you can see the positive outcomes intended from "above," and how you can work along with the process. You'll see things about the situation you didn't see before, usually including some more bits of work needed on your part that you had left out of your "first take" of the situation. You'll see the fairness and evenhandedness and the justice in it. And you'll typically be seeing the whole situation far better than those who are not making any assumption of the perfection and integrity of the Universe.

If you're the only one in the situation who is thinking, "for what greater good could this be happening," which will frequently be the case (until this planet wises up), you will be the Universe's Agent on the scene. Higher MindMat powers will be with you, so long as you continue to act for the good of all, along the lines you think the Universe has in mind, open to learning more about the Universe's intent as you go along.

If you look and listen for it, you'll see and hear synchronistic clues from the Universe in situations like that, which go past everyone else but have special meaning for you, guiding you to make the best of things.

In looking for synchronistic "winks" from the Universe in visual events around you — possible double meanings in what people say to you or in overheard conversation or in the lyrics of background music, and in the material that pops into your consciousness — you may wonder if you're acting like a paranoid schizophrenic.

People in that variation of the lowest level of human consciousness also have the tendency to read everything that happens as a special message to them. The one difference is that the paranoid schizophrenic is looking for evidence of a hidden conspiracy out to do him or her harm.

In the approach recommended here — which might be called "Noia," in contradistinction to paranoia — you're looking out for messages from a hidden conspiracy that's out to *help* you and everyone else, not do you harm.[16]

Keep an eye and ear open for helpful messages that others might not notice.

In the Noia frame of mind, if you see something you don't initially like, you say to yourself something like "there must be some reason I'm being forced to see this: perhaps it in some way mirrors something I could be doing better."

It's surprising how regularly this way of thinking *does* trigger an awareness of something one could be doing better.

---

16 In Greek, "para" means "against," and "noia" means "mind." Paranoia works against the mind, while what we call "Noia" works positively on its behalf. Writer Rob Brezsny has a similar concept he calls "pronoia" about which he has written an amusing book by the same name.

CHAPTER 37

DE-ATTACHMENT

Working against you as you strive to flow with events in the direction you divine to be intended, will be your tendency to fly into a tantrum when you don't get what you want. This is what is meant by being "attached."

When you are in this sense attached to something, you are stuck in it, vulnerable to it or to its absence.

Your attachments are perfectly normal. They are "where you are" in your process of relating to the addictions of existence.

God always gets attached in evolving mini-personality roles. You are God being attached. And God always gets past attachment. You yourself are *already in the process* of getting past attachment if you are still reading this book — chances are, you started the process before picking up this book.

We might define attachment as applying to those things that you may choose in your intellect to say you're not attached to, but when the critical moment comes, your emotions hijack your consciousness. It is your emotions not your intellect controlling your actions: you "throw a tantrum" — lose intellectual control — and your actions show that you *are* attached.

To what might you be attached in that sense?

Here's a list of likely attachments:

1. Not dying.
2. Not feeling pain.
3. Not being made fun of.
4. Not being insulted.
5. Not being emotionally hurt.
6. Not losing your loved ones.
7. Good health.
8. Good health for all those around you.
9. Being "well off" financially, being able to afford the things you want.
10. Being physically fit.
11. Being sexy.
12. Being a good lover.
13. Having a good sex life.
14. Being well-regarded/looked up to, having a good reputation.
15. Recognition in one's field.
16. Fame/immortality in history, being remembered, not being forgotten as if you never existed.
17. Making a difference in the world, making your mark on it.
18. Having a sense of controlling your life, not feeling powerless.
19. Feeling intelligent, mentally at the top of your powers.
20. Being in love.
21. Being loved.
22. Being able to trust the one you love.
23. Self-respect.
24. Children, family, a sense of community, of belonging.

25. A sense of having a good relationship with God. (Some of us would say they don't have this attachment, but I'm not sure that's ever really the case.)

26. At least for males, and some females: feeling confident that you could handle yourself in a fight.

27. Being right in all arguments; being agreed with.

28. Being talented, creative.

29. Being witty, a good conversationalist, "having a good personality," thinking of the right thing to say at the right time.

30. Being good-looking.

31. Being well-dressed for the occasion.

32. Not feeling as if you're standing in someone else's shadow.

33. Not feeling that your lover is more attracted to somebody else.

34. Achieving a high and powerful position from which to influence one's field and the world.

35. A generally hidden attachment: if at all possible, to be worshipped (or at least admired).

36. To have an interesting lifestyle.

37. Not being humiliated/dishonored, not to lose face in any situation. (Imagine the irony, a mask worried about losing face!)

38. To be happy.

39. To win all contests/competitions.

40. To be wise, understanding, compassionate, forgiving.

The list goes on but that's enough to demonstrate what a long list it is.

So here are all these potential tantrum triggers laying around in your consciousness, ready at a moment's notice to *work against* your flowing noiacally with events, getting into higher states of consciousness, having more *positive* MindMat power.

What to do about it? As already implied, the intellect alone cannot simply decide to give up attachments with any hope that this will really work.

But the intellect, working together with intuition, emotions, senses/imagination and actions *can* effect true self-change:

1. With your *imagination* supported by the rest of your consciousness team, you as vividly as possible (i.e. engaging all five *senses*) imagine getting the things you want, and the things you don't want, one attachment at a time. (You can go down my list above if you like, adding any of your specific attachments.)

   You don't just do this once, you do it again and again, over a period of time, until you find that you can live with or without your attachments.

   In cosmic reality you *are* going to get all those things someday, in this life or maybe in another. After you have them you will eventually become a bit bored with them — the attachments will "burn out." The power of imagination, with disciplined application, can get you to this future attitude in advance.

2. You can control your *actions* to the extent of your ability to do so (as if in a contest) in order to *minimize the outward expression* of your attachments, even if at first this is "only an act."

3. At the moments when your *emotions* are throwing an internal tantrum, you can hold back from acting until your "inner scope" clears.

4. In moments of reflection/*intellect* utilization, when you detect your own negativity on an issue, you can hold back from reaching final conclusions longer.

5. When you catch yourself being attached, you can reach deep down inside and ask your *intuition* to tell you if *you* really care that much anymore about the attachment.

This simple act has a surprisingly positive effect. *Just by sincerely questioning one's own attachment, one reduces it.*

No one of these "alchemical tricks" would be effective on its own, especially given the challenging local conditions. But the combination practiced over time does reduce attachment.

CHAPTER 38

WATCHING THE MOVIE

Let's say you're going to abstain from negativity, flow noiacally, use MindMat positively, imaginally burn out attachment, and do all of the other hard mental/emotional work I'm recommending here. What then? What will your life be like? How will it compare to your life now?

Let's face it, local conditions don't make it easy. We've got this long list of attachments we usually don't even know we have. We go out in the world to get our attachments satisfied, and the world blocks us everywhere.

Why is this so? The speedup in our intellectual development has made it easier for faster-adapting elites to soak up an above-average share of the fun, leaving less for the rest of us.

Simply the fact that we're all competing with each other instead of cooperating wastes a lot of available energy.

The One Being in all these different bodies, runs into Itself in a different body and doesn't recognize Itself but sees it as an "other," and competes instead of cooperating.

The feeling of daily life, even for elites, is going out defensively into a hostile world, a world determined to drag you down. From moment to moment, one is protecting oneself, fearful about something that might be taken away or never gained.

But in your future, some very different kinds of moments are going to start to happen.

Moments will come when you realize that, right then, you're just watching a movie — your life unfolding — *you aren't doing anything, it's all doing itself.* You're being moved through movements of unearthly perfection in what it is you're doing.

You see and accept the party that has been laid out for you, you like your life — why, you even like yourself.

Things that would normally get your goat now make you smile.

You feel like a transparent window — there's nothing to protect, nothing you can lose, no need to feel defensive.

Because you're "playing to God" not to the human audience, it doesn't bother you when some people don't know you well enough to like you.

You find that in the daily drama you're not even especially rooting for yourself as much as for the team — i.e. everybody — constantly seeking to "add to the net value of the Universe."

When you make a mistake, it feels okay because there's always the learning value in mistakes.

Sometimes when you look out your eyes you don't see a separate world out there — you're in a bubble, it's enclosing you and yet you're enclosing it.

And *it's all you.*

CHAPTER 39

A Vision of How It Will Be, When

It is my hope that the ideas in this book reach people who had given up God as unscientific. I haven't asked anyone to believe anything, only to open your mind to these possibilities, and to use the Scientific Method in your life, replicate the detective work, and see what you find.

The same goes for people who believe in God but fear death.

And for those who believe the future has to be dim, or that they themselves do not have an important individual destiny.

And for anyone else who is still attached, and is therefore not having a good enough time.

I hope that the Scientific Method allows all of us to discover the true nature of reality. It doesn't matter whether this book is the thing that triggers it. I know in my heart that someday the Truth will out. The Truth will be in the streets, and everyone will know it. Beyond intellectual knowledge, it will live in people's hearts, made real continuously in moment-to-moment relating to oneself, to God and to the God in everyone and everything.

How will organized religions react to this book? Each religion — with some exceptions — has tended to see itself as the only true religion. Will they continue to feel that way, and resist a scientific scenario such as this one, which validates their beliefs but also validates the beliefs of virtually all other religions? (The only exceptions

I can think of are the popular Atheism/Accidentalism/Materialism, and the rare Satanism.)

It will come down to the individual. Some clerics will welcome our view, some will fight it. This will be correlated with their level on the scale described in Chapter 21. The higher their level, the more likely they will be inspired by a view that explains how their precepts are true within a scientific (non-supernatural) context.

When the human race gets that hip, how will society change? What will happen to nations, to terrorism, to the quest for world domination by petty dictators and criminal undergrounds, and to the tendency to demonize one another? What will happen to all of the other dilemmas mushrooming around us — environmental degradation, poverty, starvation and homelessness, crime, disease, and the rest of the usual list of the world's problems?

When we realize that everyone we deal with is our self, we start to treat everybody a bit better.

> With all beings and all things we shall be as relatives.
> —Sioux Indian

What is now and has always been, as long as anyone can remember, a competitive situation, will begin to move more and more toward cooperation and synergy.

Once the spiritual reality has sunk in at the highest levels of the U.S. and other nations, national leaders will never again be able to picture themselves playing out the current scenarios in which each of them believes he/she alone is favored by God, and the rest or at least most of the rest are agents of The Devil. Nations will need a new game to play with each other, another way of relating.

With the resources they have been putting into firepower, advanced nations could become partners in the joint co-development of the less-developed countries (LDCs). These countries might be given a century to fully repay their beneficiaries, while with the help of the advanced nations reaching the latter's comfort status in just a few decades.

When most of us are walking around in higher states of consciousness most of the time, more creative solutions will be envisaged by the commanders of state and industry, globally.

Schools will emphasize individualized education. Students will perhaps be creatively queried to determine preferences and aptitudes, given the results, and then given the opportunity to structure their own unique study/work program. Schools work closely with industry to help students advance their life possibilities from early in their school career.

Young people graduating from school will have a better idea of their real life plans than kids have ever had before. They will know who they are — what their talents are — what their life is all about — their unique purpose.

People will do the work they love. Thus they will do it superbly well. Some will develop Internet-based systems to help those who are confused as to what they would really most like to do, and helps them to learn if they are capable of becoming good at it — although the new syllabi of the schools will have rendered the size of that group far smaller than it is at present These will be linked to other Internet systems — an extension of today's Linked In for example — that will connect workers with people who want their work.

Old-style advertising will have been mostly replaced by cause-related marketing. In other words, corporations and their brands will more and more advertise the actions they are taking to help America and the world — by sponsoring worthy causes, including their partnerships with schools — and less and less will they advertise already-well-known product claims and "brand imagery." The same will happen with political advertising — no more beating each other up.

There will be an expansion of the Voluntary Sector. Today we see sites popping up such as Volunteermatch.org that help people who want to donate some of their time to a worthy cause to find the organization to which they would most like to offer their time.

The amount of corporate dollars (and thinking) going into worthy causes will greatly advance those causes. There could even be enough money to house the homeless and feed the hungry, and to really rehabilitate criminals.

You'll never guess the first thing we might do with criminals. We might give them the kind of preference and aptitude tests that their schools probably didn't — and help them find out who God intends them to be.

When people get inspired by their own true mission, and can see a path to fulfilling that mission, they have no need for crime.

A big employment agency might go national, and maintain the most complete daily computer file of all the jobs in the country, all the openings, and all the potential employees, and try to match jobs and candidates using sophisticated methods over the Internet, without jobless people even having to ask them for that service.

The preceding is just a scenario. Rather than pushing specific solutions, we're merely citing examples of the kinds of creative, synergistic solutions needed to supersede human competition on planet Earth — the kinds of solutions people will start to think up once they realize who they, and the rest of us, really are.

"An ideal is going begging — the ideal of world citizenship. Milton, Paine, Hugo, Heine, Tennyson, and numberless others were eloquent in their plea for a world citizenship. Today, the basic fundamentals for the ideal exist, but we find that the ideal itself is virtually an orphan. History has almost lost its voice telling us for 5,000 years that states within a geographical unit must unite or fight."
— Norman Cousins, 1943

We've all got this self-determinism streak within us. It must have been hard for the thirteen American colonies to give up total self-determinism by forming the USA. It's hard to give up total self-determinism when you get married, but most of us find a way.

The United States of the World. It's going to happen someday, by some name.

The "states" will be sure to hold onto most of their traditional rights.

But the administration of this federation will coordinate world synergy on a level far beyond that of the present United Nations.

Perhaps it will grow out of the existing UN, pending UN performance in getting scenarios such as Third World Codevelopment to happen. The UN took the first step with the Millennium Development Goals (MDGs), an agenda agreed to by 189 nations in 2000 (and now by all of the world's countries) to free people everywhere from extreme poverty and hunger, to achieve universal primary education, to promote gender equality and empower women, to halt the spread of HIV/AIDS, and four other MDGs, all by the target date of 2015. Progress is being made. The MDG drinking water target, for example, had been met and surpassed by 2010.

You may be reading this book centuries into the future and it's all just beginning to happen in the way envisioned here.

I hope it hasn't taken that long.

CHAPTER 40

God Loves a Cliffhanger

The way the odds are stacked against us on this planet, we as a race have to move up into more continuous Flow state just in order to survive.

God wants us to win. We are not simply a race He set down here. We are Him. When you and I hurt, He feels it.

God is rooting for the ending in which we rise to the occasion.

It's a big Hollywood ending. Today's events shatter our security, portend disaster. Gunmen in schools and airports seem to echo the terrorist agenda as if the world itself were going mad. Nations run irresponsibly toy with nuclear weapons and far-range missiles. A new incurable disease rolls out through the population. Whole species rush to the brink of extinction. Nature seems to be trying to scour off the destructive human race from the surface of the planet with strange weather, tsunamis, tornados, earthquakes, huge storms. The signs of Armageddon are everywhere, as predicted in the Book of Revelations and by Nostradamus.

Just when it looks as if doom is at hand, we rise to the occasion and become heroes and heroines to save the day. We realize and act from our Cosmic Oneness and not from our competitive attachments and *self*-determinism.

That's the ending God wants, as far as I can tell.

Here's to that ending!

You may say I'm a dreamer
But I'm not the only one.
I hope someday you'll join us
And the world will live as one.

—John Lennon, *Imagine*

OUTRODUCTION

All that exists is one Being. The Being set up the game.

The Being is playing the game with independent Masks of Itself, which It inhabits.

The Being looks out the eyes of each Mask that It has given Free Will.

Our sense of identity is actually the Being.
The Being is enjoying playing your role.

It would be far less fun if the Being knew It was the Being.
The drama comes from identifying with your role.

Because the Being is all that exists,
everything is made out of the Being.
everything is part of the Being.
everything is the Being.

Space and Time are made-up parts of the game in the part of the playing board where we are currently playing through.

Nothing in the Being is Evil.
Therefore Evil does not exist.

The original meaning of the word "Evil" is "Missing the Mark," and this is a valid principle in the Being because of Free Will.

The Being Game is the Being.
There is only one thing.

Everything is taking place within one null point in no-Time-Space.
There is no distance except as the Game is Projected.

We are all one consciousness.
Ethics is simple common sense to a Mask that has woken up.

Death is Graduation.

Love makes all the sense in the world.
Loving everything
resonates with the highest parts of sucked-in Masks.

To be sucked in is to be suckered into believing the Game, not seeing that it is a Game.
Suffering Masks.

Awake Masks essay to wake up Suffering Masks.
Graduated and Original Consciousnesses essay to wake up Suffering Masks.
Enlightenment.

On the way to Enlightenment
Masks go up and down in degrees of almost waking up.

We call these "up" intervals the Observer state, which readies the mind for Enlightenment;

and intervals of Flow state where,
absorbed in non-separation,
The Mask operates on Cosmic Guidance.
This happens increasingly on the road to Enlightenment
and a lot more regularly after Enlightenment.

The Being gets seven types of fun out of the game.

And a Mask
in the part of the Game we are in,
tends to be focused in one of those seven motivations
at any one point in its life.

The Being comes back to play in the game through
"Sons and Daughters" it launches,
personality aspects of Itself,
each of whom plays the Game many, many times
while evolving up from simplest to most complex
as it recovers from the launch shock and becomes able in
stages to take control of the entire Game.

And thus be welcomed back as an active part of the
Being's awake consciousness.
This is your destiny.

ॐ

**The next two Parts are written primarily for the scientific
community, inviting them to investigate and, I predict, prove
this theory to be scientifically true and verifiable. If at any
point you find you are not enjoying these sections so much
(some of you might enjoy them even more), please skip to
page 244 for The Experiment.**

PART II

WHAT IS KNOWING?

CHAPTER I

WHAT IS REALITY? (WHY CARE?)

As this is written, the Earth is divided into arming camps, some at war now and others in danger of being at war soon. It has always been so, going back the length of recorded history. However, the weapons now include planetkillers.

This actual and potential physical war reflects an underlying war of ideas. The Ideological War is at the roots of human suffering on the planet.

There are many more than two sides in this Ideological War. Liberals are inspired by the idea of reducing human suffering by controlling the greed of the elites. Conservatives are inspired by the idea of free will. Error in the implementation of free will is the cause of suffering.

Meanwhile, most people intuitively feel that a Supreme Being who created the material world also exists. The Gallup International/Charles F. Kettering Foundation "Global Survey of Religious Beliefs and Practices," conducted in 1976 in 11 countries, found that 94% of respondents claimed to believe in the existence of "God or a Universal Spirit," i.e. a Supreme Being.

In the 2000s, even among Americans 18-29 ("millennials"), 45% said they pray daily, up from 40% in the 1980s, according to the Pew Research Center.

However, these believers are themselves divided into every possible flavor of belief.

Judaism and Islam are at war over control of their holiest ground. Ironically, the average Jew and the average Muslim know little of the specifics of their supposed ideological differences.

In Lebanon: Islam, Christianity, Judaism, Marxism, and other Ideological Elements wrestle for control of the turf. The Hindu-Buddhist-Moslem- Druze syncretism has more explicit ideas about reincarnation than most of the other Ideological Combatants. The Christian Phalangists have alternately been their allies and enemies for hundreds of years.

One might argue that these wars have nothing to do with ideology, they are wars for control of material territory, yet it seems more than coincidence that the warring factions are split neatly along ideological lines. Perhaps the ideological differences are merely excuses to distrust "the other."

Then when Malthusian population-growth pressure makes one look around for more "living room" ("Lebensraum," as Hitler called it), one knows by ideological differences whom to distrust and therefore whom to invade — even though one does not remember the specifics of the ideological differences themselves.

Real Communication about Ideology (via the mass media including social) could therefore be a potential unifying tool, since by not remembering specifics there have been mass assumptions of irreconcilable differences. Thus, when real communication takes place about ideological specifics, there is at least a chance for realization that greater ideological agreement exists than disagreement.

It is hard to imagine the armed camp phenomenon being permanently dispelled by any other means, absent such ideological communication.

We've given up talking about it.

Despite the apparent need to get underlying ideological issues out into the open, most of us have long since given up talking about it. The main reason for avoiding communication on these issues is that they are emotionally touchy and intellectually hard to talk about, and so attempts at cross-ideology communication often quickly end up in irritation, frustration, and a change of subject.

Many children in America, Europe, and elsewhere are taught to avoid bringing up religion and politics in polite conversation. The UN is the apparent forum for world communication, and rarely through this or any other forum does our Global Society communicate on a philosophic level.

The attitude is that "everyone else is too pigheaded and uptight" to successfully carry out inter-ideology philosophic communication. Therefore, "since such communication is hopeless, let's just try to co-exist peaceably on the more superficial day-do-day levels, while agreeing to tacitly disagree on philosophic issues, and let's just not talk about it anymore."

A paranoid might look at this as a worldwide conspiracy to avoid reminding oneself of the most profound questions — What Is Going on Here? Who Am I? What Is My Purpose?

By avoiding these questions in order to not put a spark to the tinderbox world of resignedly closed-mouthed ideologically-isolated armed camps, we allow the tinderbox to dry out even more. Soon it may reach the point of spontaneous combustion.

Even if this non-communicative attitude were not certain to lead us to doom, it has already led to a philosophic sere emptiness in mass culture and in most individual lives. The media communication streams of the culture, programming most of the waking hours of most individual lives, politely avoid probing the specifics of apparent ideological conflict (the notable exceptions being hate radio and its more recent TV counterpart, some of which masquerade as a news channel, which exacerbate differences rather than seeking resolution), while reveling in the sensuous details of actual physical conflicts, including natural and other physical disasters. **Most people have no idea what it is they live and die for.**

The philosophic vacuum-cleaner is everywhere and does not exempt the one remaining superpower. In the USA, it is obviously impolite, gauche, and too embarrassing to talk about anything beyond the day-to-day material world.

One of the reasons for this embarrassment is the behavioral inconsistency of most of the believers. People who do not always act consistent with their belief are just not sure — by their actions they are wavering between believing in a Supreme Being and believing in a material-only Universe.

The Gallup International study found that the proportion of Americans (USA) who believes in a Supreme Being is above the world average. Yet many of these are wavering believers, embarrassed by their wavering, and therefore preferring not to be reminded of anything beyond the material realm other than escapist horror or superhero entertainment.

The wavering of believers is itself a function of the materialist bias of the prevailing culture and its media streams. Most scientists (although very few of the most famous and influential scientists) who make mass high technology possible proceed from a positivist/materialist bias: all that counts is the measurements. We cannot help but be influenced by the trickling-down of the tacit materialist philosophy of the generators of our civilization. In the serious moments of our media streams, the sensuous material world is all that is shown, all that counts. Anything "beyond" is already kooky or going to turn kooky.

Someone growing up in our culture is subtly influenced to distrust anything but the material world, and to distrust anyone cleaving to an ideological label of any kind. At the same time most individuals have intuitions of a Supreme Being, and nurture these intuitions in their children. "Supreme Being Talk" becomes something kept inside the family unit and the walls of their places of worship, publicly communicated as little as possible except among those discovering that they cleave to the same ideological label. Even within one's own religious group conversations rarely venture into the philosophy of their religion.

Yet another impetus to ideological reticence rippled in from the apparent fadeout of Sixties idealism. In the Seventies, more serious Sixties people went underground, attempted to compromise, or tried to helpfully steer the system from within. In their wake the less-serious Sixties idealists were left to play out their acts, make fools of themselves, and be predictably derided during the next two decades by the prevailing materialist culture.

In the aftermath of these public spankings, intuitions of the metaphysical ("beyond the physical") became even more firmly closeted.

The division between Science and the Intuition of a Supreme Being is overdue for reconciliation.

Science is allowed in the light of day, while the Intuition of a Supreme Being must skulk behind children's doors.

Science and the Intuition of a Supreme Being are probably the two greatest achievements of the human brain on this planet so far. While our best minds strive to reconcile alternative models of the subatomic world, isn't it time to schedule and reach for similar reconciliation between Science and the Intuition of a Supreme Being?

Two Different Ways of Using Our Brains

In the last 6000 years we have learned how to use our brains in the Scientific Method and in the Religious Method. It might go further back but without written or even oral linguistic record keeping, earlier periods are a matter of the unknown.

The Scientific Method has proved itself in that time to be supreme over the Religious Method for gaining Knowledge and Technology.

The Religious Method has proved itself in that time to be superior over the Scientific Method for gaining Ethical Wisdom and Understanding.

History is a record of increasingly-dangerous imbalance favoring scientific Knowledge and Technology, at the expense of equally-dangerous widespread deficits of Ethical Wisdom and Understanding.

What if we could use our brains both ways at once?

CHAPTER 2

Epistemology =
What Is Knowing? How Can We Know?

At its root, the word "know" means "to see."

We primates trust vision much more than our other senses. Dolphins apparently trust hearing more than vision (not being primates), and so the root of the dolphin word "know" might mean "to hear."

Leaving aside the species-specific question of which perceptual sense or senses happen to be trusted the most — sight and/or hearing and/or smell and/or touch and/or taste — the idea of knowing comes down eventually to perceiving something for oneself.

This root idea of "knowing" as "perceiving for oneself" has gradually been forgotten, and today the word is only occasionally used with its original meaning, "I experienced this myself." Most of the time "I know" now means "someone told me this."

This corruption of the word "know" had already occurred by the time The Golden Age of Greece arrived. The ancient Greek philosophers developed a branch of philosophy to deal with this problem. They called it "Epistemology" from the Greek *episteme*, meaning literally "plant-stems" and metaphorically "to stand up to." Epistemology is the branch of philosophy (incidentally, the latter word means "the love of knowing") that is concerned with the question of "how can we know?"

Again, this was not a question before the word "know" (in various languages) began to mean more than "see." It only became a question (i.e., "The Epistemological Question only arose") as the word "know" started to sometimes, and then increasingly often, mean something else — namely, "someone told me this."

The first question of Epistemology then, was the question of "Can we know something without experiencing it directly, that is, if someone tells it to us?"

To this day, this seemingly simple question has not yet been answered to everyone's satisfaction. Instead, differing schools of thought have grown up, each with a different answer to this question. Two obvious schools arose almost immediately:

Empiricists: In its purest form, this school says that to know, we must experience something for ourselves. If someone tells us something, we may choose to believe it, but we ought not to claim that we "know" it.

Authoritarians: This school says that we can know something by hearing it from a qualified authority, without having to experience it for ourselves.

Of course, the only real difference between these two "primary" schools of Epistemology is their definition of the word "know." In the twentieth century, we have generally learned not to argue about definitional differences, but rather to simply adjust for them.

If these two "primary" (i.e. "predictable from the causes") schools of Epistemology were the only ones to arise, the matter might have ended there. But some "secondary" schools arose that could not have been easily predicted by studying the original questions. These schools principally include:

Rationalists: This school says that we can know certain things *a priori*, i.e. prior to sensory experience of it, by use of the rational mind. This position is argued in a variety of ways, often based on the fact that the human mind is a part of nature, and thus if there is any basic logic to the structure and process of the Universe, it would seem to have to be mirrored in the inherent logic of the human mind.

Mystics: This school says that we can know certain things directly without use of the five physical senses, and without use of the rational mind. Mystics claim to receive such knowledge directly, as if by another sense.

These were the important "secondary" schools of Epistemology. By the secondary schools combining with one or the other of the primary schools, a spectrum of "tertiary" ("admixture") schools developed, including:

Crypto-Authoritarian Empiricists: While this is not a school publicly espoused by anyone, some scientists who claim to be empiricists are, from their actions and words, actually more devoted to sticking to the beliefs of their particular authority figures in Science than they are devoted to sticking to experimental evidence.

Mystico-Empiricists: This is another not-publicly-espoused-by-anyone school, but it contains some of the most important scientists in history, such as Einstein, who "knew" that "God could not be playing dice with the Universe."

The direction of Einstein's work was derived from certain patterns he "saw" in the Universe, in what we would categorize as a "Mystic" way based on the definitions given above. He then proceeded to do experiments to empirically verify these Mystical perceptions.

When empirical experimentation appeared to point consistently in the direction of random processes at quantum (subatomic) levels, Einstein stuck to his Mystico-empiricist perception over pure empiricism, adamant that "The Old Man who Einstein knew would not shoot craps with his elegant mathematical creation."

Obscurantists: We assign this name to those who doubt whether knowing is possible at all. (Obscurantists clearly don't know what the word "know" means, or they would realize that they are doubting whether or not the eyes exist.)

Reductionist-Empiricists: This is a school that grew up as a reaction to the Mystic school. The Reductionist-Empiricist school promptly laid down the law that Empiricism meant knowing by the five physical senses only, and that anything outside this realm could not be subject to empirical knowing.

Reductionist-Empiricists can logically argue that since the word "know" came from our having eyesight, the word ought not to be applied to anything outside the realm of our eyesight. What they forget is that the blind can know using their other senses, and as mentioned earlier, the human emphasis on sight over the other senses (as recorded in the etymology of the word "know") merely reflects our primate ancestry.

Once one admits that sight is not the only way to detect "objective" (i.e. sharable with other observers) information, the need arises for a more-sophisticated modern definition of "knowing" divorced from the compulsion of our primate genes. This definition might be:

To know = to detect an event that is in principle detectable by other observers.

Thus, one can know (without the eyes or any of the five senses) that one "has a mean streak" by looking inside oneself so deeply as to profoundly understand a behavior pattern that is in principle detectable by other observers. Interestingly, these other observers will verify the knowledge using their five senses, although it was not initially gained using those senses. We are driven to the conclusion that there are other operative senses beyond the five senses, which can predict results that will be verified by the five physical senses.

The requirement of verifiability by other observers is offered as a part of the proposed definition of "know" in order to ensure that the information detected by the individual observer is "objective," i.e. the information can "stand up to" scrutiny by other observers. We will recall that the word "Epistemology" comes from this very idea of "standing up to" and of such "verifier-observer" scrutiny. Thus, the ideas of objectivity and verifiability are already implied in the concept of Epistemology.

The Reductionist-Empiricist would argue that the ultimate detection instruments must be the five physical senses.

The Pure Empiricist would ask to see detectable proof of this compulsive need to limit detection gear. "Why do so?" the Pure Empiricist might ask. If the mind can detect without the five senses, and make predictions later verified by other observers (with or without the five senses), why would we deny that the predictor knew something?

A Pure Empiricist might realize he or she does have certain self-knowledge, not gained through the five senses, that is predictable of one's own future behavior in ways empirically verifiable by other observers later, using only their "five-sense detection gear."

Debate Time

Reductionist-Empiricist: I take exception to your last statement. I say you have no self-knowledge except by analyzing your memory of behavior. Your memory just stores what came in through your five senses. All knowledge is still based on the five senses.

Pure Empiricist: You still haven't proven it to me. I detect internal feelings in myself that are not merely memories of the five senses but responses to these memories. This feeling information is very helpful to me in understanding myself, and in predicting my own behavior. If I left out these detections, my predictions of my own behavior would be less verifiable by other observers using their five senses. This differential in verifiability convinces me that there is real objective knowledge in those feeling-detections that I get without using my five senses.

Therefore I realize that I have more detection gear than the five senses. And the fact that you almost convinced me not to pay any attention to some of my real detection gear scares me, sobers me up, and makes me want to be very careful and very much the Pure Empiricist before being convinced by anyone to in any way "shut down" or "pay no attention to" any of my built-in detection/knowing gear. I don't know how many senses I have, and I won't accept your *a priori* insistence that there can be no more than five detection/knowing senses — in fact, I think you're no Empiricist at all, you're a Crypto-Rationalist with your *a priori* limitations!

(Sound of fighting)

Once we open the door to other "detection/knowing gear" beyond the five physical senses, the Mystic walks in and sits down. The Reductionist-Empiricist and Pure Empiricist, now rolling around on the floor biting each other's ears, see the Mystic and turn on him to eject him.

Reductionist-Empiricist: Get out of here you madman —

Pure Empiricist: Grrr ?!?!?!?!?!?!?

Something weird has happened. The Pure Empiricist locked eyes with the smiling Mystic, something passed between them (!), and then the Pure Empiricist froze in his tracks before grabbing the Mystic's throat.

Reductionist-Empiricist: What's the matter with you? Help me get rid of this nut before he drives *us* nuts!

Pure Empiricist: (Unfreezes, sighs deeply, falls back into a deep armchair, and finally, smiles.) No, I'm afraid we're going to have to let him stay from now on.

Reductionist-Empiricist: From now on?! What do you mean?! That's the direction of insanity.

Pure Empiricist: No, he's got us. Once I accepted the idea that we might have other valid detection gear besides the five senses, he knew we'd have to let Mystics into the Empiricist Club.

Reductionist-Empiricist: Into our club! What are you, crazy?! Mystics aren't Empiricists.

Pure Empiricist: We thought they weren't. We thought they were making up "Rationalist-type daydreams" and convincing themselves or pretending that this information was received, rather than originating with them. They always said they were following our Empiricist principle of "perceiving for themselves," but that they had discovered other senses. We never believed in those other senses — you Reductionists convinced us to feel that way.

Reductionist-Empiricist: So what's changed?

Pure Empiricist: I've finally gotten sophisticated enough to debate the point with you, and now I realize that Reductionism-to-Five-Senses is not intrinsic in Empiricism; in fact it's an *a priori* bias and therefore Crypto-Rationalism — not Empiricism at all! While Mysticism comes in the door once I accept detection gear with objective verifiability beyond the five senses — and now I do — emotional introspection is at least one other such valid sense. Out with you!

(Reductionist-Empiricist is booted out the door, which then closes.)

(Sound of door pounding and on the other side, gnashing of teeth. Reductionist-Empiricist kicks door once and then stomps away.)

Pure Empiricist: So Mystic, tell me about all these other senses. Do you carry a list?

Mystic: The way to discover your other senses is empirically, yourself. I can help you set up experimental situations, which will tend to mirror the situations I experienced that triggered in me the realization of these other senses.

The Mystic goes on with a description of an ancient Pure Empiricist approach to introspection, which he calls "Meditation."

We leave the Empiricist clubhouse now, to return to The Main Thread. What is knowing? How can we know?

We propose the following answers:

- Knowing means detecting information that is in principle verifiable by other observers (we call such information "objective").

- There is an as-yet-unknown number of human detection senses for such objective information. (The minimum number would appear to be six: the five physical senses, plus emotional introspection.)

A Pure Empiricist approach is recommended. While being the oldest school of Epistemology, Pure Empiricism is also uniquely qualified to deal with the present situation in which we find ourselves with an unknown number of senses — in that any other school would tend toward *a priori* expectations/biases regarding the number of our senses.

In effect, the Pure Empiricist school of Epistemology is least biased in that it steadfastly refuses to accept any constraint prior to proof of the compulsion to accept that constraint.

- Using the Pure Empiricist approach, actual empirical experimentation via the Scientific Method appears to be necessary in order to determine the list of human senses that detect objectively verifiable events.

- Until such experimentation has successfully circum-navigated the human sensorium, each of us intelli-gent/sophisticated human beings should live our lives without explicitly or implicitly believing in unproven constraints to our number of senses. Such biases would tend to be self-limiting, i.e. we would tend to ignore and thus be cut off from sensory channels giving us objec-tive information were such channels to exist where we didn't expect them to.

Debate Time Again

(A crowd of Epistemologists of varying stripes, using a battering ram, crashes through the door into the Empiricist's Club.)

Reductionist-Empiricist: I take exception to this whole line of argument. You seem to be implying some extrasensory perception, but you haven't proven it!

Pure Empiricist: But no one has disproven it, and I just don't want it to be rejected without being disproven! I've got no axe to grind about proving or disproving it, but the rest of you do! You've all got a heavy ego investment in your particular bias!

Mystic: Not me. I started out like you. It's just that I've been a Non-reductionist Pure Empiricist longer than you have. When you've experimented introspectively without prejudice for as long as I have, you'll be using as high a percentage of your sensory equipment as I use of mine.

Mystico-Empiricist: I've got no axe to grind either. I'm just like this Mystic here, except that he prefers his introspective senses, while I like to use my five physical senses through the Scientific Method in order to verify the hunches or "intuitions" I get through introspection. I think I represent the most sophisticated epistemological viewpoint of those represented here — I think the Mystic and the Pure Empiricist are at earlier stages of epistemological evolution into: (ahem, sorry if it sounds less than humble) me.

The Mystico-Empiricist runs to the blackboard and rapidly draws a diagram:

TRUTH

Mystico-Empiricism

Non-reductionist Pure Empiricism (Mysticism)

Rationalism

| Reductionist-Empiricism | Obscurantism | Crypto-Authoritarian Empiricism | Authoritarianism |

CONFUSION

Mystico-Empiricist: Let's assume a "Truth vs. Confusion Scale." Let's say that in this diagram, "up" is toward Truth, and "down" is toward confusion.

Obscurantist: Who's to say which is better?

(Other philosophers gag and sit on the Obscurantist.)

Mystico-Empiricist: Let's say there actually are numerous introspective senses that gather valid, predictive information. After all, this could be the case. Let's say that a number of seekers after Truth adopt differing styles to get to Truth — that's all of us differing epistemologists.

Based on the initial assumption I've just made, for the sake of argument, that there are valid introspective detection channels, the Reductionist-Empiricists among us would tend not to get to Truth. Therefore, in this diagram they would move downward.

(The Reductionist-Empiricist becomes obstreperous and is similarly gagged and sat upon.)

Anyone who is secretly attracted to Confusion — that is, the Obscurantists — will obviously tend to also move downward toward the Confusion they seek.

Crypto-Authoritarian Empiricist: I can see why your diagram has the Obscurantists and Reductionist-Empiricists going down, but why me?

Authoritarian: And why me? Why, I was philosophizing when most of you hadn't been born yet.

Mystico-Empiricist: Both of you are really just Authoritarians as far as I'm concerned — and what I think is wrong with Authoritarians in general is your preference for reliance on authority-figure observers, in place of perceiving for yourselves. But in this specific instance, your preference is deadly. Remember our assumption: the possibility we are investigating is that there are valid introspective senses. If there are such senses, by relying on other people, you Authoritarians are likely to learn how to use these senses long after most everyone else. Meanwhile, by their constant practice of introspection, some Rationalists are likely to stumble on these introspective senses and to become by their use Non-reductionist Pure Empiricists, i.e. Mystics. Other Rationalists will not stumble on these senses, moving downward in the diagram into Confusion.

Pure Empiricists, unfettered by unwarranted constraints, will eventually also stumble on whatever inner senses exist, also then becoming Non-reductionist Pure Empiricists, i.e. Mystics.

Then, eventually all Mystics will tend to evolve into Mystico-Empiricists in order to gain the power of the Scientific Method.

If there is an Epistemological style more closely suited to reaching the Truth than Mystico-Empiricism, we haven't yet discovered it. After all, Einstein was a Mystico-Empiricist, and who is smarter than him? In Mystico-Empiricism you get the Scientific Method, no unwarranted assumptions, and potential inner senses too (if they're there, you get 'em, but we don't insist on fooling ourselves if they're not there).

(The Mystico-Empiricist waves his Mystico-Empiricism flag and jumps up and down in the routine of an M-E cheerleader.)

Mystic: (Points out to The Reader.) Look, guys, you see that person looking in on us? (The others look around, see nothing, and stare at the Mystic as if he's crazy. Mystic realizes it's pointless to talk further with them and addresses The Reader directly.)

Do you get the point of this whole exercise?

Reader's Advocate: (Pops into being out of nowhere.) Of course The Reader gets it.

Mystic: Yeah? Well, what's the point, then?

Reader's Advocate: Well I'd say it's implied that there was some kind of an epistemological drift in our culture that suckered us average people into unconscious Reductionist-Empiricism, out of which this chapter is trying to jar us. The author wants us to be Pure Empiricists, to leave room for the possibility that introspective sense(s) can lead to Truth.

Mystic: I'd say you got it. What's your reaction?

Reader's Advocate: I'm always willing to open my mind further, in an area with so little evidence one way or the other. Perhaps there were biases present in The Reader's mind before, but after reading this chapter, any such biases are gone forever.

Mystic: You think so? I'd say that's an unproven assertion — and an improbable one. Based on my knowledge of inner spaces, when you consciously change attitude, there are remnants of the old attitude that "retreat into the hills of the unconscious" and continue their operations from there. I'd suggest that The Reader be on the lookout for these counter-revolutionary forces within himself/herself as we continue the expedition.

Reader's Advocate: No doubt The Reader agrees. Let's proceed.

CHAPTER 3

Seeing Reality vs. Seeing a
Representation or Model of Reality

Epistemologists for the last 2500 years have argued as to whether or not we are to allow detection gear other than the five senses into our discussions of reality.

They have also argued for just as long about whether or not to allow even the five-sense detection gear to stand as witnesses of what reality is.

Philosophers from Aristotle to Plato down to Hume, Berkeley, and Kant all realized that, since we perceive the world not directly but through our senses, we do not see the world "as it is" but instead we see it as it is represented somewhere in our body by our body's systems.

Earlier philosophers differed as to where they thought these representations appeared: some thought the heart, some the liver, some the pineal gland, some the brain. Modern empirical Science has verified that those philosophers choosing the brain were the best guessers (or knew by some sense other than "the basic five").

Regardless of where in the observer's body these representational processes take place, the fact that they must take place somewhere inside of us raises the question, "How do we know that our five senses are giving us an accurate picture of the world out there?"

It also raises another question: "How do we even know if there is a world out there?" It might be, as postulated by Bishop Berkeley,

that "only He exists and the rest of the world is a figment of His imagination." Or that you, dear Reader, might be the only thing that exists, and all this stuff out here represented to you by your "bodily sensory processes" originates in those "bodily sensory processes." But they aren't "sensory" at all, they are "imaginal." This position is known as Solipsism: "Only I exist."

The fact that other people are able to curtail the freedom of most active Solipsists (most people who believe that only they exist tend to wind up in mental institutions) is:

- One good reason not to espouse Solipsism.
- A sign that either:
   A. Something other than the Solipsist exists, because it acts independently of, and even contrary to, the Solipsist's will.
   Or
   B. The Solipsist has parts of himself he can't control at the moment, or he is playing a game pretending that to himself.

Because of the "B" option, there may be no way to absolutely disprove Solipsism.

However, if it can be shown that there is in principle no way to ever either prove or disprove a proposition, the proposition isn't false, it's meaningless. Solipsism appears to be one of those things that can never be either proven or disproven, i.e. no matter what happens a Solipsist can always declare the rest of us to be in his head. Therefore we feel justified in declaring Solipsism meaningless as a description of reality.

Before we go on our way, leaving Solipsism behind us in the dust on the path to reality, let us give it its due as a "lens" that each of us can look through and that gets us to use our minds in some new ways. You may want to close the book and your eyes for thirty seconds and pretend as hard as possible to yourself that you really are a Solipsist, and that everything is a figment of your imagina-

tion. You may feel various intuitions such as "Solipsism is not right
— I just feel it," or "Solipsism isn't right, but it's got a piece of the
answer in some way I can't quite put my finger on."

The intuitions we are stimulated to experience by such "lenses"
as Solipsism justify the existence of such "nonverifiable-thus-mean-
ingless" ideas: they may nonetheless be utilitarian.

Having set aside Solipsism, we are still left with the question
of whether our five senses are giving us an accurate picture of reality. Plato's image of cavemen watching shadows on the cave wall
and inferring what reality is all about gives you some idea of Plato's skepticism regarding sensory information. Other philosophers,
Hume for example, have been more bullish about the senses, pointing out that instances of, say, optical illusion, do occur, but are rare
and are significant only as exceptions proving the rule that usually
the senses do not lie.

Twentieth-century Science has now revealed that, in fact, our
five senses do not give a particularly accurate picture of the texture
of reality. It turns out that the real world is a dance of vibrating
energy and most of what we are looking at is empty space — and
yet we "gestalt" it all as hard, all-filled-in-solid, and not vibrating.

Although our five senses hide the real texture of reality and
make it seem denser than it is, the five senses get us through our
lives helping us to not run into objects too often, and so it is obvious that the senses are, in fact, validly predictive of the spatial location of things in our local environment. It's equally obvious that we
shouldn't rely on our five senses in judging the texture of reality.
Whether or not we can rely on our five senses, therefore, depends
on what we're going to rely on them for. They're good at spatial
location, bad at texture, and we won't necessarily know "going in"
whether they will be valid for judging any specific aspect of reality
— we'll have to test them for predictivity.

Predictivity is the ultimate Truth gauge. Since we can't always
trust our five senses, what's our infallible rule for knowing Truth
from Falsity?

IIf we make a prediction based on information, and that prediction comes true, we can provisionally regard the information on which the prediction was based as true, pending further such prediction-testing. If we make a prediction based on information and that prediction fails to come true, we can provisionally regard the information on which the prediction was based as false, pending further such prediction-testing.

There is a potential flaw in the predictivity Truth gauge (PTG): between the information and the prediction is the interpretation of the information. True information can lead to a wrong prediction if the interpretation louses it up. So the PTG is only sold with a special exploding collar to be worn by the person who will be interpreting the information to be tested.

Actually, the way around this potential flaw in the PTG is to exhaustively test alternative interpretations of the basic information, to see which interpretations are most predictive — those are then assumed to be the right interpretations. "PTG WAIT" (predictivity Truth gauge with alternate interpretation testing") is in fact the Epistemological approach of Quantum Physics, the pinnacle of modern Science. Thus what we are recommending here as the best way to proceed, not knowing which information/interpretations to trust, is the way that quantum physicists proceed.

And for good reason: in closely inspecting the texture of reality, these subatomic physicists moved off the human sensory scale and have ever since been forced to rely entirely on instrument readings (machine senses). They were justified in being suspicious of both their "detections" and their "interpretations." Thus, the only way for them to determine Truth from Falsity was by using predictivity as a test gauge, with separate predictions based on alternate interpretations if any.

We started out looking for reality, wanting to "know" what it is. So far the big question has been "how are we going to know if we're right or not?" In the previous chapter we questioned whether we could trust anything other than the five senses in putting together our description of reality. In this chapter we considered whether we could even trust those five senses in assembling our description of reality.

The conclusion we have reached parallels the approach of Quantum Physics: if it predicts, it's right. This means there need be no restrictions as to the source of the description of reality: the source might consist of five-sense information, instrument readings, inner-sense information, or a mix of any of these: the test is still the same — does the description predict?

Reader's Advocate: Excuse me, but a "description" can simply be a mathematical equation, and it might predict quite well and keep lots of physicists happily predicting the splatters of subatomic particles — but both the game of mathematics and the game of splattering subatomic particles mean very little to the average person. I thought you were going to give us a picture of reality that anyone could visualize.

Mystic: You're saying you want a description that both predicts and depicts?

Reader's Advocate: That says it.

Mystic: Our objective, too, is a description of the Universe that the average person can visualize — not just a mathematical equation, or a concept that cannot be visualized.

However, here we must pause and consider the additional criterion we have just introduced: what is the a priori justification for insisting that the Universe must be visualizable by the average human being? What if, in fact, it isn't? We would then be forced to create a simplified visualizable model of the Universe to meet our two criteria: predictivity and depictivity. So long as the simplified model did predict, we'd be happy with it, even knowing (or suspecting) that the visualizable picture was not the real thing but a simplified version.

But wouldn't we then always long for the real thing? And wouldn't we continually strive to make visualizable models that were also less and less simplified, closer and closer to the real thing (which we could check based on increased predictivity)?

Admittedly at this point we are discussing not only Epistemological but Aesthetic criteria as well: the adding of a visualizability-by-the-average-person (or "depiction") criterion brought in this entirely Aesthetic criterion not necessitated by Epistemological criteria (which were entirely satisfied by the "predictivity" criterion alone).

The danger is that our Aesthetics might damage our Epistemology. For example, we might sell ourselves on a very-visualizable description.

Those fluent in higher math are willing to settle for an equation, and for them there is no tradeoff to be made between Epistemology and Aesthetics: they are both lined up.

But for those of us without this fluency, we crave a description that we can get our minds around. Let's assume for the sake of argument that the most-predictive visualizable description we can provide at any given moment is less-predictive than the most-predictive non-visualizable description we can give at that moment: in such a case, we might let the mathematician/scientists use the most-predictive description and the rest of us could use the visualizable description — though that could tend to get the rest of us in trouble.

Kant speculated that Time and Space were not really qualities of the Universe, but qualities of human detection gear — that we added Time and Space as constructs in order to be able to represent the Universe to ourselves.

If Kant is right, then in fact we have "sold ourselves on a very visualizable description," not out of Aesthetics but out of the nature of our bodies.

Even if Kant is wrong, we know since Freud that humans have a tendency to repress information they don't want to be reminded of. To repression (remembering only what the mind wants to remember) modern psychology has added selective perception (seeing/hearing/etc. only that which supports one's concepts) as further reasons why we as humans should be wary of our Aesthetic preferences influencing our objectivity in attempting to accurately depict and predict reality.

Another form of perceptual screening discovered in the twentieth century is linguistic: we humans tend to selectively perceive in line with the language we use.

All of these different selective perception mechanisms appear, from the most recent work in psychobiology, to be related to the brainstem's Reticular Activating System (RAS). The RAS is designed to screen out all but the most relevant information coming into the brain from the five senses, letting only a tiny fraction of a percent of the input enter consciousness. When the RAS is temporarily turned off or down (e.g. by LSD), consciousness experiences information overload, dramatically demonstrating the evolutionary purpose of the RAS.

Still, the RAS can distort our awareness of reality through the above-mentioned selective perception mechanisms.

What this portends in the context of our search for a predictive visualizable description of reality is that we'd better be prepared for our models to become lenses: that is, we're going to begin (as if by magic) to see and experience the world looking just like whatever model we prefer!

In the next chapter, we're going to talk with two characters, each of whom thinks that the other one is RAS-hallucinating the world to look just like the model he's obsessed with — the Mystic and the Materialist.

CHAPTER 4

The Materialist Lens
and the Mystic Lens

Although Science and Philosophy often seem to be going off in two completely different directions, in the long term they are working together to culminate the search for the ultimate nature of reality.

Some would oppose this assertion, countering that the work of Philosophy is utterly irrelevant to Science. If this irrelevancy were indeed the case, then no scientist's work would ever cast new light on the earlier work of any philosopher, and vice versa.

That Philosophy and Science are in fact connected efforts, intrinsically relevant to each other, may be seen in a little-noted relationship between the works of Einstein and Kant.

Again, one of Kant's main intuitive propositions was that Time and Space are constructs of the human perceptual system and do not directly inhere in external reality in the same way they appear in our perceptual model.

Einstein's Theory of Relativity indicates that the sequence in which events take place does not exist in reality; that such sequence exists only in the perception of a given observer; and different observers can see the same events taking place in different sequences (depending upon the direction and velocity of movement of the observers and events relative to each other).

This particular Einstein theory has been repeatedly verified by empirical measurements (astronomical and subatomic), which are accurately predicted by Einsteinian Relativity, and which are less-accurately predicted if Einsteinian Relativity is presumed not to exist.

What is now the Law of Relativity within codified modern Science verifies Kant's intuition about the unreality of Time.

Thus given the proper emphasis of Science upon predictivity, Philosophy is obviously of relevance to Science to the extent that the intuition of philosophers sometimes predicts later scientific verification of natural law.

The real difference between Scientists and Philosophers is that a Scientist is focused on a tighter field of information and seeks exactitude within that tighter field, whereas a Philosopher is focused on a much broader information field and seeks to detect broad patterns rather than exact details. The two approaches can obviously be helpful to each other — especially when simultaneously embodied within one investigator such as Einstein.

Let's look more closely at the "unreality of Time" as correctly predicted by both Kant and Einstein.

What Science now knows is that event-sequence does not have absolute reality. Instead, event-sequence has relative reality — the specific event-sequence has reality only relative to a specific observer.

Curiously, at the small fraction of light speed that humans move around in, your perception of event-sequence and mine are identical. Only up at near light speed do we see different event-sequences.

It is as if the Universe were designed to give a perfect illusory appearance to its slow-moving inhabitants, while allowing only its faster inhabitants to see the true nature of reality.

The perfect illusory appearance shown to the slower-moving observers makes them think that Time is an absolute external reality. The faster-moving observers can tell from their own direct experience that Time is relativistic, that is, each observer has his/her own real Time, and these separate real Times are connected to each other in complicated ways. However, all of these separate observer-timelines do not fuse into a single objective timeline — there is no such thing.

Time, therefore, is an "observer-mediated effect" in the Universe, but to slower-moving Universe-ites ("as if not to worry them") it appears convincingly to be an "independent-of-observer effect."

Whether or not this insight into the nature of Time is of any practical significance to us slow-movers, it does reveal that Science has now confirmed the suspicions of philosophers that "reality as it appears to us" may give highly misleading clues to "reality as it is."

Thus, whatever our senses may tell us about the "obvious nature of reality," we must be careful to suspend judgment.

When this was said by the Vedas, Thales, Plato, Aristotle, Hume, Berkeley, Kant, and many others throughout the past 3500 years or more, the average person considered it an interesting possibility but dismissed it as having no relevance to his/her life. In our present age, with scientific support, the matter is due more serious consideration: it may indeed have significance as to how one views the Universe and consequently as to how one runs one's life.

There would be less immediate significance to the "sensory illusion" if we all saw the same "sensory illusions." However, this is not the case: there are at least two popular "sensory illusions" seen by us as Earth humans. Millions see the world through Lens A, millions see the world through Lens B, and millions switch back and forth.

We call the two lenses the **"Materialist Lens"** and the **"Mystic Lens."** Here are the main characteristics of the two types of perceptual display.

A 1975 survey[17] (worthy of replication today) indicated that about half of all adult Americans have experienced the Mystic Lens at one or more times in their lives. However, the Materialist Lens is clearly the current dominant perceptual style in the West, while the Mystic Lens remains most common in the East.

---

17 "Are We a Nation of Mystics?," Andrew Greeley and William McCready, *The New York Times*, 1975. Sample size = 600.

On both sides of the world, the Mystic Lens appears to be a more common perceptual style in childhood, becoming less and less frequent as we grow up. This suggests that the Mystic Lens might be the style we are born in, and the Materialist Lens might be an effect of the Materialist Western Culture that has molded both sides of the world for centuries.

Freud theorized that the newborn baby sees the world as a sphere around him/her; he/she is the center of this sphere, and everything in the sphere is connected to him/her as a part of him/her.

Freud further theorizes that this perceptual style (which we call Mystic) breaks when the baby for the first time does not get immediate gratification, signaling to the baby that some of the sphere is "not baby" and needs to be dealt with, and thus must be separate. At that point the ego forms to deal with this new "other," and the baby begins to see separate objects (in the "Materialist Lens" style).

While it is true that the images formed on our retina are upside-down, a newborn baby's brain has not yet learned the complex task of processing visual information. Perhaps when the optic part of the brain kicks in, making the images right-side up, the process of separation begins.

Besides being common in childhood and in the East, the Mystic Lens is also more frequently reported among long-term meditators, among the more intensely religious, among those that have survived near-death experiences, and among those that have experienced chemically-induced altered states of consciousness.

The world as perceived by Mystics and others who see through the Mystic Lens bears an uncanny concurrence with the world as described by Quantum Physics, at least in some particulars.

The Mystic sees the world vibrating, which Quantum Physics verifies is the case. The Mystic sees it as not solid, again verified by Quantum Physics — most of the atom is empty space. The Mystic sees that everything is made of energy — which Einstein told us in his famous $E=mc^2$ formula, matter is just a special type of energy — in effect "very dense energy." The Mystic sees light coming out of all things. In fact, all atoms radiate photons of light (as electrons "fall to nearer orbits around" the atom's nucleus). Through the Materialist Lens one's senses are unquestionably fooled on these four points (Vibration, Solidity, Substrate, and Luminosity in the table below).

AS SEEN THROUGH THE

Particulars	MATERIALIST LENS	MYSTIC LENS
Substrate	Everything appears to consist of matter.	Everything appears to consist of energy.
Vibration	One sees most objects as not vibrating.	Everything is vibrating.
Solidity	One sees objects except liquids, semiliquids, gases, and flames as hard and solid.	Nothing is solid, and the tactile feel of "hard objects" sensorily emphasizes not that they are "hard" but that they are "tight" (energy field).
Luminosity	Most objects do not appear to be luminous (light-emitting).	All objects emit light and sparkle to varying degrees. Human beings may be seen as surrounded by multi-colored "eggs of light."
Causality	Many if not most events appear to come about randomly.	Everything appears to stem from a cause.
Attention	Attention tends to be focused externally in front of oneself.	Attention tends to be spherical, i.e. focused diffusely all around and within oneself.
Separateness	Everything appears to consist of separate objects.	Every object appears to be connected to, and to inter-permeate its neighbors; objects are mutable cells in a unitary, mindlike containing continuum.
Consciousness	Only human beings and higher animals appear in any way conscious.	Everything appears to be conscious; you sense that an object is paying attention to you.

Particulars	MATERIALIST LENS	MYSTIC LENS
Over-Consciousness	One does not sense the attention of a Universal Consciousness upon oneself.	One senses the attention of of a Universal Consciousness upon oneself.
Powers	Because one perceives one's mind as separate from matter, matter cannot be directly acted upon by one's mind.	Because all exists within a mental continuum telepathy and precognition appear as additional (possibly hallucinatory) senses, and telekinesis appears as an additional (possibly hallucinatory) power.
Numinosity	Most of the time one does not sense any particular drama in the moment.	Most of the time there is a sense of poignancy at the meaningfulness of the moment in relation to other moments.

Science now proves that the special perceptual style of Mystics is more accurate than the more common Western style today in the latter four particulars, a fact that makes us look more closely at the other particulars wherever Science has not yet definitively spoken.

On the issue of Causality, Einstein and Aristotle agreed with the Mystic sense that "Everything that occurs has a cause" (Aristotle) and that no event occurs randomly ("God does not play dice with the Universe") (Einstein). However, Bohr and Heisenberg, and perhaps half of the twentieth century's quantum physicists, disagree with Einstein and Aristotle in this regard, believing that randomness is a property of the Universe. Ultimately, the hard scientific evidence to prove or disprove randomness has yet to be presented.

Regarding Attention, the Mystic Lens style of paying attention in all directions, including internally, would seem to be a better strategy from a survival standpoint than paying focused attention to what is in front of oneself. Such a practical survival benefit might in fact exist; but this has nothing to do with determining which, if either, lens gives us the more accurate picture of reality.

Are we separate or connected? On the particular of Separateness, Science is today on various fronts discovering evidence of connectedness where previously, separateness was presumed to exist — this is becoming a current trend in scientific discovery. A few examples:

- The photosphere of the Sun encloses the orbits of all the planets; in effect, we are living inside the Sun.

- All forms of life and possibly inanimate matter are enclosed and connected by fields that we know next to nothing about.

- Separated subatomic particles that once contacted each other appear to still be connected in that they exchange information at faster-than-light speed (one interpretation of Bell's Theorem). An alternative interpretation of experimental evidence that avoids superluminal (faster-than-light, "tachyonic") movement is that distance is an illusion.

Arrayed against these tantalizing but not-yet-final scientific soundings is the persistent Materialist Lens perception that "separateness is obvious and why bother talking about it?" The answer is that to those in the Mystic Lens, "connectedness is obvious so why bother talking about it?"

In a Materialist-Lens-dominated country such as America, the next question might be: "Why bother responding to those in the Mystic Lens?" Even in such a country it would be an impolite question. We need remind ourselves of how many intelligent people have viewed life in the Mystic Lens style, including the Mystics who wrote our Bible, and including Jesus. To dismiss the potentiality that the Mystic Lens style is the more accurate is to beg the question.

We are just now coming to the particulars on which the two lenses are farthest apart: Consciousness, OverConsciousness, Powers, and Numinosity. To those seeing through the Materialist Lens,

- the suggestion that a rock or an electron is conscious may seem ridiculous (Consciousness);
- they will sense no God paying attention to them (Over-Consciousness);
- they will tend to be properly skeptical of telepathy, tele-kinesis, and clairvoyance since, as a consequence of the Materialist Lens, they do not experience these things themselves (Powers);
- and the tendency of Mystics to be awed by the Presence of God all around them (Numinosity) appears "too emotional to be rational" in the thinking-over-feeling-oriented Western Materialist culture.

Thus it is these last four particulars that make communication between Mystic Lens people and Materialist Lens people particularly difficult.

Do Mystics see Quantum Reality, i.e. what Quantum Mechanics physicists mathematically model but cannot "see"? If so, why do they see everything as conscious?

Reader's Advocate: Perhaps the Materialist Lens is a distorted perceptual model the RAS forces us to see, in order that new impressions not create psychic dissonance with our existing beliefs. And perhaps the Materialist Lens was created and transmitted by our culture. And perhaps the Mystic Lens is merely another RAS-distorted perceptual-model, but simply one that was developed by an earlier culture than our own? In other words, what if everybody is hallucinating?

Mystic: Then the way to see reality is to stop prejudging in any way. Clear out all beliefs. Pick hidden assumptions, like lice, out of your language and thought patterns. Then observe.

Materialist: And I bet you then continue to see exactly as I see.

Mystic: And if you have no expectations, I bet you eventually begin to see somewhat as I see.

Materialist: Hah!

CHAPTER 5

ENDING THE WAR BETWEEN
RELIGION AND SCIENCE

All Religion has in common two things:

1. The Intuition of a Supreme Being, or Beings, or Ground of Being (i.e. an impersonal "Force").

2. The desire to enter into a better relationship with (the Latin *religare* = "yoke up to") this Supreme Being or Beings or Ground of Being.

Science has come to mean lithe explanation and prediction of all events by the fewest possible laws; deducing these laws by the refinement of intuitive hypotheses. and refining these hypotheses via the process of testing each hypothesis in controlled experiments, to see if the measurements taken do or do not corroborate this hypothesis.

On the face of it, given the above working definitions, what is there for Religion and Science to fight about?

It would seem as if Science is in the business of testing intuitive hypotheses, and now Religion comes along and has not one but two of these intuitive hypotheses to test!:

(a) that a particular kind of Universal Entity (or Entities) exists; and

(b) that human contact with this Entity (or Entities) is feasible.

Thus, one would expect Religion and Science to be happy to find each other:

Religion: Oh Science — it's a miracle that I've found you at last! Now you can test — and possibly refine — my two key "hypotheses"! What great proselytizing props your reports will make! And if you do refine my "hypotheses," what wonderful new things will I find out about God and about our destiny? How exciting! Perhaps you'll even improve "yoking" techniques and get us all even closer to our Maker... (Religion ecstasies out).

Science: Religion, it's really a pleasure to take your business. (Besides the fact that all this military work is depressing...) Now we can put our tools to The Big Questions at last! This is surely the worthy destiny for which Science was created, and toward which so many good men and women have worked for centuries... (starts toting up the bill for much higher-energy atom smashers, radio telescopes, etc.).

Somehow this was not the way that Religion and Science greeted each other (on our planet and in our recorded history, at least — perhaps there are more intelligent civilizations in which Religion-Science team-ups are the norm). What happened here? Why the war? Let's look at an overview:

The Relevant History

Back before written history, before the great Monotheistic (One God) religions, there were primitive religions that had grown up as muddled admixtures of the two key hypotheses, mashed in with all manner of superstition. The human mind had not yet discovered the tools of analytical thought with which to separate the two key hypotheses from the immense jumble of superstition. Hence, blood sacrifices were a main feature of our planet's real "Old Time Religion."

Then there came a succession of Great Teachers who began the process of the creation of modern religion. But this process has not come very far, as each Great Teacher's work was subsequently overlaid with updated facets of the original primitive religion. Thus, Christianity today is not what Jesus taught, but a combination of Christianity with elements of all prior primitive religions of Afro-Eurasia; Islam is not what Mohammed taught, nor Judaism what Moses taught, but in each case the religion is a compound of the original teacher's teaching with elements of the prior primitive Afro-Eurasian religions.

"Great Teachers" may be a misnomer. Certainly these individuals were Great Thinkers, not only for their own day but for ours as well. From their words and ideas we may be further entitled to assume that they saw through the Mystic Lens, and were trying to teach others:

(a) to play nice, and
(b) how to see through the Mystic Lens for themselves.

But "Great Teachers" implies that at least some students were able to embody the teaching. Some people are great at doing a thing but not at teaching it, while others may be better at teaching it than at doing it. Or perhaps in more fairness we have a situation where truly Great Teachers dropped in amongst a paucity of Great Learners. At any rate, as Science began to develop on this planet it ran into "not just Religion, but Primitive Religion". Hence the enduring adversarial relationship, down to our present day — but not necessarily beyond it.

One of the first sticking points was the audacity of Science in its willingness to consider the possibility that Earth might not be the center of the Universe. Primitive Christianity was attached to the geocentrist notion even though Jesus never mentioned it. The

Primitive Christian Church threatened Galileo with torture and death for dabbling further with Copernican Heliocentrism (sun-centered solar system). Galileo happens to have been, if not the first Scientist to begin to use controlled experimentation, then certainly the one who impressed the idea of conducting experiments on the next four centuries of Scientists. The Galileo case may have been the Fort Sumter of the Religion-Science War.

In the Primitive Religion style, the Primitive Christian Church facing early Science was attached to having everyone believe exactly one way on a long list of particulars (which went far beyond the two key hypotheses and far beyond anything Jesus ever said, to include in a submerged/changed form practically every element of the long-running primitive religion group).

Primitive Religion probably takes such a defensive stance because of the undeveloped analytic powers of the leadership. Since the religion cannot easily be analyzed into separate parts ("hypotheses"), it must stand or fall as a monolith. In retrospect, a more sensible approach would have been to place great emphasis on the two key hypotheses plus everything Jesus said, and to have been willing to reconsider anything else.

The latter strategy would have avoided the loggerheads that occurred over heliocentrism and over evolution, neither of which were put down by Jesus, and neither of which are in conflict with the two key hypotheses.

Science for its side was not perfect in the relationship. Most scientists to this day, like most other people, have completely missed the point of all Greek Tragedy: success breeds arrogance.

And Science has been spectacularly successful for the past four centuries. So successful that, beside today's Science, Primitive Religion looks like just what it is, Primitive. The average person who, due to modern culture, knows almost nothing about either Science or Philosophy or Religion (except for Primitive Religion), looks at the humiliation of Primitive Religion alongside Science and thinks, "Well, all Religion must be like that — mere superstition," and turns away, back to modern culture.

In its success, Science has occasionally wandered over the border into Philosophy, and being untutored there, has sometimes allowed its hidden Parsimony Aesthetic to get in the way of its Epistemology. In the next chapter we'll decode the latter tongue twister, and relate how Science's hidden Aesthetic value system has undermined Religion, and how this can now be discontinued in the case of non-primitive religion. What is non-primitive Religion? Religion that (1) limits itself to the two key intuitive hypotheses (there is a Supreme Being, and It can be contacted) and (2) proceeds to test these hypotheses using Mystico-empiricism, without clouding things up by locked-in *a priori* ideas of any kind (fish on Friday, the Trinity, not lighting matches on Saturday, praying in a certain direction and/or at fixed times of day, not eating certain things, etc.). One can continue to obey all of those rules out of Aesthetic preference without being tagged as primitive by this author. We seek only to separate out the pursuit of Truth from all else, and it is that pursuit alone on which this book is focused.

CHAPTER 6

The Hidden Agenda
Sometimes Afflicting Science

Science has at times suffered from a confusion of values. On the one hand, it is a search for Truth. On the other hand, the scientific community tends to respond enthusiastically *only* to hypotheses that are "elegant"/"parsimonious"— i.e., reflecting an economy of ideas, even in the explanation of complex events. This "Parsimony Bias" is the hidden Aesthetic value system in Science, and confusion of values has been introduced in Science over the issue of "Truth vs. Parsimony."

A philosopher, William of Occam, enunciated the Parsimony idea in a logical rule for hypothesis-formation called "Occam's Razor" — in effect, the Razor says, "Use the fewest variables that describe all observables." Science loved Occam's Razor and put it right on top in its bag of tricks.

Science was at its rudest to Religion when Science took out Occam's Razor and used it to chop off the two key hypotheses:

Religion: (Nauseous, horrified, Hellishly unhappy) Why did you do that?!

Science: Well, old boy, you see, we really don't *need* those two hypotheses to explain all the observables. We can explain all the observables with just four variables (the four forces — electromagnetism, gravity, the strong and weak nuclear forces) or with just one (a unified field theory). Why add superfluous variables like Supreme Beings? Occam's Razor, you know.

Religion: (Retches.)

Here's what Religion could have said, but didn't:

Science: (Starts to leave.)

Religion: Wait a second, you fool... (wiping mouth).

Science: (Stops) Huh?

Religion: What if there just happened to be a Supreme Being and He didn't agree with Occam's Razor as a way of designing things — what if He liked ornamentation, for example?

Science: Well, then we should discover evidence of superfluous structures and processes.

Religion: Like the human appendix? And the redundant processes observed throughout nature, for example, that allow a person to retain his/her entire memory despite destruction of much of his/her brain by a hand grenade, for example, suggesting redundant storage? (Note that diseases that attack the brain more strategically are quite capable of wiping out memory.)

Science: Hmm... maybe.

Religion: It seems to me that if Whatever created this Universe had the same Scottish parsimonious Aesthetic as William of Occam, It would have left out the whole Universe. But let's forget that argument for a second. Let's go back to your claim that you don't need God as a hypothesis — then how do you explain the existence of the Universe?

Science: Some kind of bootstrap operation. For example, it could have all come out of a white hole.

Religion: Isn't that one hypothesis?

Science: Sure.

Religion: So by getting rid of the God hypothesis and replacing it with a "bootstrap" hypothesis you're not really increasing the Parsimony of your solution — there's still one hypothesis for creation in either case. Seems to me that you can't really claim Parsimony as your motivation for ousting God.

Science: Well, it isn't Parsimony as William of Occam thought of it. Think of it as "modern, relative Parsimony" — it's not only the number of variables, it's also "how hard a given variable is to swallow."

Religion: Sounds very subjective to me.

Perhaps a dialog might have been started on either or both of those points, i.e. "Why Parsimony at all?" and "Why fake Parsimony?" But neither Primitive Religion nor Primitive Science had the Philosopher-Logicians on their teams. Scientists passed remarks about not needing the two key hypotheses of Religion, which the average person heard and assumed meant that the wisest people in the world, the Scientists, had disproven Religion at last.

Another misadventure by Science into Philosophy further undermined Religion in the beginning of the twentieth century. Logical Positivism was all the rage in Philosophy, and Science mirrored this with its own Operationalism: in both cases the idea was to avoid using words that did not convey pictures, so as not to waste time babbling meaninglessly. Science went further in its version of this idea. Whereas Philosophy was satisfied that a hypothesis was meaningful if it was, in principle, "verifiable," i.e. testable, Science on the other hand often demanded that in order to be meaningful, a hypothesis had to be testable *by measurement techniques currently available or soon to be available.*

This was quite a problem to Religion: it had no idea how to specify measurement techniques acceptable to Science, since Science had always insisted on "objective, external yardsticks and meters" checkable by multiple human observers, rather than on human senses or human introspection not subject to direct checking by another observer. How to get God to show up on a dial? In its second major rudeness to Religion, Science in the twentieth century dismissed the two key hypotheses not only as unnecessary — but as meaningless.

Again the average person caught dribs and drabs of the byplay, by this time filtered through the considerably-distorting lens of the media, and the average person was now utterly convinced that, playing by the pure rules of Science, Religion had been discredited — not only the primitive-superstition parts of Religion, but also the two key hypotheses.

This was an unfair process. An unwitting public was allowed to throw the baby (two key hypotheses) out with the bathwater (Primitive Religion) based on rumors of opinions by scientists that did not even play by the pure rules of Science. (Neither Parsimony Bias nor Immediate-Testability Bias ought to be considered part of the pure rules of Science, whose search for Truth ought not be deflected by the Aesthetic of Parsimony nor by the Pragmatic preference for sooner-testable-hypotheses.)

Meanwhile these hidden agendas in Science began to attract negative attention in their own sphere. Scientists began to guard against "Reductionism" as Science realized its own preference for elegance/simplicity and attempted to keep this preference from impeding the attainment of Truth.

In the field of Psychology for instance, Skinnerian Behaviorism had declared that one's consciousness was a mere "epiphenomenon" with no causal control over one's own behavior. Although introspection had never been allowed into scientific evidence, most scientists outside psychology trusted their own introspection to tell them not only that Skinnerian Behaviorism was a ludicrous embarrassment to Science, but also that the Science that allowed such theory to arise must have some deep-seated problems to work out.

This was and is indeed the case throughout Science. The deep-seated problems stem from the personal rewards sought by most scientists — status, perks, and mostly the budget and freedom to do their chosen work. These rewards usually come to those that rouse positive scientific opinion — here it helps to have "Parsimony," and to those that produce commercially or militarily significant results — here it helps to have "immediate testability." Thus the real world concerns of flesh-and-blood scientists are what tend to cause such hidden Aesthetic and Pragmatic agendas to creep into the pure Epistemology of Science.

Ironically, the behavior recommended by the "Great Teachers" for improving connection with the Supreme Being and for improving visibility through the Mystic Lens, appears as if it could help scientists stay focused on Truth without regard for personal side agendas such as status, budget, and perks. This is ironic because, if true, scientists are being obstructed from getting to the possible right medicine by the disease itself.

Current countertrends in Science represent a healthy groundswell. Despite such human side agendas as might exist, the pattern of current discoveries is away from Reductionism: the window of Science has been opened wider, allowing more of the Truth to come in.

In a search for simple base-building-block particles to the Universe, Science hoped that quarks would be the simple component underlying everything, reducing everything to one or two or at most three types of particles. Thus far, half a dozen different types of quarks have been found, with another half-dozen antiquarks. And the family of all subatomic particles catalogued thus far has become a regular zoo with about five dozen species — with more species being discovered (or created) every day as Science uses higher and higher energies in its atom smashers.

With Bell's Theorem, Science has opened its mind to two possibilities previously excluded, either Action-at-a-Distance or Faster-than-Light-Communication based on the fact that particles once connected appear to retain connectivity forever. Action-at-a-Distance — the idea that something can be moved without touching it in some way — has been excluded for about 2000 years longer than Faster-than-Light-Communication (the speed of light limit to the speed of all motion in the Universe was an Einstein contribution). And Action-at-a-Distance was what Einstein hoped to avoid with his "geometric" theory of gravity, and what modern Quantum Physics attempts to avoid with its "exchange of particles" model for every interaction or repulsion. Science's willingness to reconsider such classical prejudices brings the discipline into courting range of Religion.

Here again, beyond Primitive Religion are the Philosophically and Scientifically meaningful two key hypotheses of Essence Religion:

(a) A Supreme Being exists, and
(b) the possibility of communication with that Being exists.

Science is challenged to design the tests by which to verify or ultimately disprove these two key hypotheses.

If forms of individual behavior and introspection turn out to be the only ways to test the two key hypotheses, Science will remain ignorant of the Truth to be found in these ways unless some scientists follow the individual behaviors, and report back. The public would be able to reproduce the experiment and so skeptical readers of the report would have a direct means of alleviating their uncertainty by doing the experiment themselves.

This may turn out to be the way it goes.

CHAPTER 7

ALL OF THE DIFFERENT DESCRIPTIONS OF THE UNIVERSE CAN BE RECONCILED

Imagine a student going through a library, scanning thousands of books, somehow getting the gist of each one instantly and going on to the next.

S/He stops and rests. Each book persuasively puts forth an idea that seems eminently reasonable to his/her mind. S/He has heard that some of the authors violently disagree with each other. The ideas as they come out of the books may or may not disagree with each other — it is hard to tell. But whether these ideas fight each other or not, s/he doesn't know, or how they combine with each other. How would their authors react to each other at a cocktail party? S/He does not know.

What if all language-packages describing reality contain some germ of subjective/objective (one or the other or both in each instance) Truth, and it was the sudden recognition of that Truth that motivated someone to say it? What if the underlying greater Truth is itself the unifying factor that makes all of these different language-package descriptions align with each other? What if, after eliminating factual errors, all statements in the World Library could be computer-logic checked against each other for internal logical consistency, and a single worldview projected from the consensus?

This angle of thought might be dubbed "Fusionism": the suspicion that the great bulk of all statements align in a more-complicated reality — but appear to conflict only when looked at in the context of a presumed simpler reality.

What if remarkably few of the words ever uttered in the world truly disagree, once understood in the context of the unexpectedly-complicated multilayered reality that really exists?

CHAPTER 8

KEEP AN OPEN MIND SO YOUR RAS DOESN'T UNNECESSARILY LIMIT YOU

The most recent work in Psychobiology suggests that the Reticular Activating Structure (RAS) of the brainstem controls the selection process determining which few, of the myriad things happening-to-and-around-you each second, you will notice.

The RAS is apparently programmed to select for things that tie to survival-oriented memories, e.g. we notice animals quickly because they are remembered to be potentially dangerous.

The RAS is apparently also programmed to reduce stress by ignoring things that don't fit into our worldview. We tend to see only the things that reinforce our worldview.

Now that Psychobiology has discovered these functions of the RAS, more and more psychologically-sophisticated people are realizing that they cannot afford to let their minds begin to close on a subject until all the evidence is in. If they do start to lean toward a tentative position on any subject, their RAS becomes programmed to fully convince them of that tentative position by more-selective noticing.

As one becomes more sensitive in introspection, it is possible to observe how one's perceptions and experiences change as one's beliefs and expectations are modified.

These tricks of the RAS may create a self-fulfilling loop as regards the two key hypotheses. For example, those who believe that Science rules out God may tend to see the world they expect to see, and may screen out awareness of a real, scientifically-valid Ground of Being that could otherwise be contacted; while those who believe in a particular type of primitively-supernatural God may also screen out such contact with the real God.

Obviously, when one is searching for Truth, one does not want to settle for any such mere self-fulfilling hallucinations of the RAS. Therefore, awareness that each of us has a RAS must make us *intensively introspect to find out what our own beliefs are*, which are probably now distorting the reality our brain presents to us, and must make us *intensively concentrate to convince ourselves even at deep unconscious levels* to drop those beliefs, so we can see the real world as it exists without RAS censorship.

CHAPTER 9

WE ARE NOW READY

The Two Key Hypotheses are intuitively compelling for most of the world's population. Nevertheless, for thousands of years we have lived with Primitive Religion. Our descriptions of God have been allegorical: a scientific description has somehow never been attempted.

Semi-scientific descriptions abound, and form an extensive body of literature and tradition known collectively as "the occult" ("hidden"). Each of the major occult descriptions seems intuitively as if it could easily hold a piece of the Truth (as does every religion, primitive though it is).

In Chapter 7 (Part II), we introduced the thought that seemingly-conflicting ideas might merge into non-conflict if the right angle can be found from which to look at them.

What follows is the description of the Universe that is most real for me. It fits the known scientific facts, including the latest work in theoretical physics (while speculating considerably further than the limits of the scientifically proven).

What is unusual is that it is simultaneously in agreement on key matters with most major religious and occult descriptions of the Universe. Thus it is a synthesis that reflects the Fusionism idea: a synthesis reconciling Science and Religion.

PART III

THE THEORY OF
THE CONSCIOUS UNIVERSE

CHAPTER I

SUMMARY

The Theory

The following is a précis of the theory we have expounded in this book, which we hereby submit to the scientific community.

There is only one of us — the One Mind-Computer that always existed. That one mind built a projection system out of its own consciousness software — a system that allows The One Mind to project out and live through a created being... and through many of these at once. The One Mind can put out as many overdubs as it wants, and has filled the Universe with created beings — each one a part of the original mind. When we die, we remain aware, and go back into the consciousness software to play another role in the scheme of things. Ultimately a conscious death is when we will be able to definitively confirm the Theory of the Conscious Universe. In the higher states of consciousness one is able to remain conscious during the transition into death. In the lower states this is not the case. These are our hypotheses.

Summary

The present-day inability to reconcile Science and Religion causes a kind of unrecognized dissociation in individual consciousness. The ensuing behavior pattern is focused on the here and now, individual day-to-day dramas involving money, sex, power and negative feelings. In the information overload of the invention acceleration culture triggered by written language just 6000 years ago, we put aside the Big Questions as to the real meaning of life, and for expediency and getting along with others, we subscribe to pre-packaged religions including Atheism/Accidentalism/Materialism.

The individual, when cued to respond on a spiritual level, shifts gears for brief periods into his/her spiritual domain. The ability to do this for brief periods masks the problem.

Speaking from that reserved space, the individual typically expresses a belief in God usually through the religion in which he/she was brought up, often with Deistic overtones that soften the supernaturalism of the native religion with a tinge of scientism. The Deistic overtones however paint the possible God as either potentially something like An Impersonal Force, a verb, a hologram, or in other ways characterize the potential God as non-anthropomorphic, indifferent rather than benevolent, and quite possibly never reachable, understandable, or connectible to our minds.

We are apparently quite willing to live with this condition. The focus on the here and now is seen as a positive thing. Not knowing the Truth about God or the nature of reality is not a concern. Who cares? What possible difference could it make?

Plato and earlier philosophers (including Kabbalists, Vedics, Taoists, Buddhists and others) formed the basis for Science by establishing logically that whatever reality is, we cannot apprehend it directly through our senses; that what we apprehend is the product of the interaction between reality and our sensory apparatus. Science today is based on Logical Positivism, which derived from this original "Platonic" point of view. Science makes statements that predictively or postdictively explain the observables, and these statements coalesce into theories. No claim is made as to what really exists beyond the observables except as useful constructs, i.e. useful fictions. Science has leaked into the popular culture in one aspect as a willingness (invoking Heisenberg, who put a scientific limit on our ability to ever know everything, specifically to know both the position and the movement direction of a particle) to never know what lies beyond the useful fictions that help us manipulate technology in the day-to-day here-and-now headspace. Who cares?

The counter side to Logical Positivism seemingly has not occurred to anyone. If we can never know what lies beyond our senses, then what comes through our sensorium to us is all we can ever know. This is the same as saying *the only thing we can know that for sure exists is consciousness.* You are reading this through your consciousness. I am writing it through my consciousness. To paraphrase Descartes, who was tramping around very close to this notion, "Thinking is going on and so therefore consciousness exists." Rene assumed that he himself was the thinker and that therefore he had proven his own existence. We submit this went a little beyond the evidence — hence our restatement above.

If we wish to reconcile Science and Religion, a logical approach given what we have established so far is to say that if God exists, God could be a consciousness — not just "could be" but "quite probably could be" since the only thing we can say exists for sure IS consciousness. Science would not be in a very good position to fight this since Science cannot deny that consciousness exists. In fact its very bedrock, Logical Positivism, makes the existence of consciousness axiomatic by implication.

Speculating logically that God exists and is a consciousness, it is also conceivable that the consciousness each one of us calls his or her own is in fact God's consciousness. Picture a faceted consciousness where one point of view (POV) sees everything in every facet and other POVs see only one facet (or even many facets but not all facets). This kind of setup is not unknown and in fact is redolent of a networked computer system. The Master POV has a password and sees all files. A lowly POV can only see his/her own files. POVs in the middle range see some (perhaps later, many) files. Perhaps POVs start low and then are allowed into more and more files/facets until they are re-established as congruent with the Master POV, adding a new side to the personality/memories of the Master POV. If a computer can do this, then why not a consciousness? They are similar in that they both process information. Perhaps they operate according to some common rules.

No matter how many experiments one runs in the world, no matter how many observables that superstring or any other materialistic (i.e. consciousness-excluding) unified field theory of everything weaves into a single equation, no matter how much we find out about matter and energy — so long as we continue to know little about consciousness, we will never discover the true nature of reality, if the foregoing speculation happens to turn out to be true. We will just have a clear picture of the plumbing. The true nature of reality, if our Theory of the Conscious Universe turns out to be true, will only be discovered within our own consciousness. The method: tuning to higher POVs within ourselves, which perhaps can allow us to expand our POV into more facets/files. From the writer's experience, it certainly allows us a more intimate connection with the Master POV. This tends to de-dramatize the money, sex, power, negative feeling here-and-now headspace so tacitly valued by virtually all of us day to day. Hence there is a major disconnect. One would have to risk everything to follow this Theory of the Conscious Universe, placing lesser value on the win-lose mentality.

If our theory is true then how far we have come from our Source and how wasted are our lives. How much more exciting life could be if we seized the internal connection we have with That Which Runs The Universe, and risked loss of the trivia that impel us day to day.

What we are attempting to do in our Theory of the Conscious Universe is to totally respect and utilize the language and methods of Science to investigate consciousness by means of working hypotheses.

Key aspects of the theory with action implications in the day-to-day (how readers will act if this theory inspires them) include:

1. Remembering and being excited moment-to-moment by the awe-inspiring scope and unknownness of what we are part of;

2. Realizing (or trusting) that "my consciousness" is just the way "The One Consciousness" appears from "where I am right now," one tends to stop thinking as a separate self and instead thinks as part of a larger Whole;

3. Realizing (or trusting) that "since I am part of The One, it is not in The One's Own Best Interest for me to be hurt" (a One Consciousness Universe is naturally benevolent)

4. The moment-to-moment focus is more likely to be "loving God" and "feeling the Oneness" and "being strength for the team" rather than winning/losing;

5. Clues will be noticed as if coming from unseen allies;

6. One will focus on what one's real questions are, with the assumption that once posed they will be answered;

7. One will tune into the future one wants, expecting support from the Universe;

8. One will realize that there are smarter and not-so-smart voices within oneself and will devise ways to discriminate among these, tuning the POV "upward" (our book *MIND MAGIC* is a tool for exploring the operational aspects of this tuning among internal POVs);

9. There will not be a dissociation between the spiritual side of the self and the dominant day-to-day side;

10. To the extent that one is happier with the results of this new mindframe, as a result of more of one's actions being positively reinforced by the surrounding Universe and its inhabitants, this will tend to raise the chances of the Theory of the Conscious Universe being the true explanation.

CHAPTER 2

BACKGROUND

In the dawn of our present civilization, the earliest scientist-philosophers wondered about the essential nature of the Universe. They considered many possibilities that became enduring themes, still unanswered:

> Is every event determined by what has gone before; or, if there is freedom from such determinism, how does it arise?

> How did the Universe begin?

> What, if anything, exists beyond the border of our senses?

> What is the relationship of the individual to the Universe?

> Does some aspect of the individual survive death?
> Which is more basic to the Universe, matter or mind?
> Is there an omnipotent omniscient Being?

> Modern Science has not stopped wondering about these questions but has allocated most of its time to working on smaller ques-

tions, where scientists can see ways of using its tools of experimentation and measurement to find answers. And consciousness has been virtually ignored by Science. Even psychology has fallen into the same trap of working on things that can be measured and counted (by consciousness) that exist in the consensual space between us (as seen by consciousness).

Not everything that can be counted counts and not everything that counts can be counted.
—William Bruce Cameron, sociologist

Some of this modern work has cast alluring light on some of the questions — without reaching any final answers. For example, regarding the question of determinism, patterns in scientific data suggested to some (such as Heisenberg) the existence of non-pre-determined random elements, to which Einstein responded, "God does not play dice with the Universe."

(Intriguing that Einstein's Relativity of Time is in relation to The Observer — we'll come back to this.)

As another example, the generally-held "Big Bang" theory ostensibly explains how the Universe began. Of course, it does not explain how the stuff that came together to cause the Big Bang got there in the first place. Some scientists use terms like The Original Superparticle to describe what was there before the Bang, but putting a name on it does not answer the question of the Universe's origin.

Logical Positivism is the epistemological philosophy of many modern scientists. This position states that whatever there might be beyond the senses is unknowable — which justifies not spending any time on it. Statements of a spiritual nature are labeled meaningless by this philosophy. This modern position harkens all the way back to Plato (who came to a different conclusion) and even earlier. The issue of being trapped in our senses occupied the thinking of innumerable philosophers including Berkeley, Hume, and Kant. By definition, experimentation and measurement can never show us results that we are physically unable to see. Therefore, in keeping with its measurement/quantification goal, Science has allocated its time elsewhere.

Where Science has concentrated its experiments and measurements most fruitfully — from the standpoint of shedding light on (although still not answering) the ancient questions — is at the subatomic level. Here for example we have found that the apparent solidity of objects is indeed a ruse to our senses: those apparently solid objects (including our own body) are mostly empty space (between the nucleus and the circling electron shells there are huge gulfs of "nothing") — and the objects seem to "push back" when we touch them not because of their solidity but because of the electromagnetic interactions between the object's components and our own.

What we used to think of as solid matter has been revealed to be one phenomenological aspect of a more insubstantial substance of matter — energy, the basic substance of the Universe.

Although distance is a self-evident aspect of the explicate (visible) order of the Universe we perceive through our senses, as Plato and many others suspected there may be a more basic implicate (not visible to us, from our level, but visible from the view of the whole consciousness of the Universe) order to the Universe that we are not equipped to perceive, in which distance does not exist. Action at a distance, such as in the cases of magnetism and gravity for example, troubled scientist-philosophers from Aristotle to Newton. How could one thing move another thing without touching it? The modern general explanation is that there is touching through the exchange of particles.

One of the most profound uses of modern scientific experimentation and measurement is the work that led to Bell's Theorem. This work shows that particles, once they have been in close contact, appear to remain in instantaneous (faster than light) communication when they are separated — so that if one is caused to manifest as a wave, the other will do so; or if the one is caused to manifest as a particle, the other will do the same. One of the possible explanations for this phenomenon is that, on a deeper level than we can perceive, distance does not exist.

These intriguing and as-yet-uncompleted probes of modern Science into the fringes of the perennial questions at least validates that the perennial questions have not lost their relevancy.

However, from the standpoint of modern culture, these original questions have indeed been shelved in the back of the mind — so far back that it is a conundrum. Why would these questions, the first we asked when we learned to think — both as a race and as individuals — sink so completely out of sight for most of us at most times?

Partly it is because we have learned to think of these questions as unanswerable. This is convenient given the time scarcity created by the current world culture. Partly it is because we have schismed our minds into the scientific/rational domain versus the emotional/ spiritual domain — and we have consigned the existential questions to the latter world, where we have subscribed to a specific religion to work out all those things for us.

And partly it is because on an intuitive level we have tacitly assumed the answers. On the basis of the mood of modern Science, we have assumed that the Universe came about accidentally and so did life and intelligence. The argument is that given enough time this accidental self-ordering of random matter-energy is not so unlikely. The rational/scientific part of each of us (the dominant part in our culture) has tacitly bought this argument. It is this rational/scientific part of ourselves that most of us allow to run our lives, except on certain occasions when we feel it is appropriate to allow our emotional/spiritual side to come to the fore and take control — such as in relating with a loved one.

This schisming into separate domains is what has allowed us to make irrelevant what had once been burning questions. We have conveniently slid into an operational procedure whereby the questions no longer matter. On an abstract basis this is regrettable since it was these questions that propelled us from natural animals into our present state of human development.

On a practical basis it is tragic because the schismed society supports intramural competition among the Religions, and a wall between all of them and Science. Would the same tensions exist in the Mideast and in many other places if, for example, Science proved that all Religions were essentially true?

Purpose

It is our purpose to propose a scientific theory for the explanation of the Universe. The specific theory also reconciles Science and all of the world's Religions. It is not the only possible explanation for the Universe but it is the explanation the writer intuitively feels to be the true explanation. In the following, our theory is applied to each of the cosmological questions raised here and elsewhere.

Definition of Terms

COMPUTER
Any system, composed of any substance, that processes information.

CYBERNETIC SYSTEM
A computer programmed to be self-regulating, e.g. a thermostat. The term was coined by Norbert Wiener.

INTELLIGENCE
A cybernetic system of a certain level. The term can be defined so that most humans and very few animals qualify, e.g. the ability to write one's name. Or it can be defined so that increasing numbers of animals qualify. The choice of how to define the term can therefore reflect one's own prejudice. The point is that intelligence is a slid-ing scale. Our personal prejudice is to credit all living things with a degree of intelligence and we suspect that manmade computers will one day qualify to be considered intelligent. Psychology defines intelligence as speed of learning but based on that definition today's manmade computers could qualify as intelligent. The term needs

to be operationally defined for each context but our most general meta-definition would be speed of learning within a self-aware system. An important objective correlate or measure of intelligence within a self-aware cybernetic system is wisdom — the capacity to make choices/decisions leading to the greatest satisfaction and the least regret.

CONSCIOUSNESS, SELF-AWARENESS
Any cybernetic system that is aware of itself. A cybernetic system of a certain level of intelligence permitting recognition of its own existence.

LIFE
Any cybernetic system that is capable of self-reproduction and has at least the potential for consciousness. That is, certain members do achieve consciousness during their existence.

BIOCOMPUTER
Synonym for "Life."

CHAPTER 3

CONSCIOUSNESS AND COMPUTERS

A Preliminary Thought Experiment

Moore's Law observes that the power, speed and what might be called the "intelligence" of computers has in recent times been doubling every 18 months. If this continues, then in about 20 years computers will be about 4000 times as "intelligent" as they are today. In 30 years they will be 4 million times as intelligent as they are today. In 40 years they will be 4 billion times as intelligent as they are today. In 50 years they will be 4 trillion times as intelligent as they are today.

During this time, computers in humanoid robot bodies can undergo intelligence testing against human norms. This testing might reach a point in the next half century (and if not, certainly at some point if the human race continues on a reasonable track) where such android computers might be assigned to undergo that most grueling intelligence testing we call everyday life.

Such a computer might be given a certain amount of money (or whatever is used in its place by that point), clothes, and a resume of its training and expected job qualifications — and sent out identified as a computer to make its way in the real world.

If we run the scenario forward into a probable future in which the human race is neither destroyed nor slowed from its course in the investigations of Science and materializations such as technology, computers could conceivably surpass human intelligence.

If humans and human-level-intelligence computers set their minds to it, they could conceivably create computers of yet greater intelligence, which could then add their intelligence to the creation of still more intelligent computers, and so on, ad infinitum.

"What If" Scenarios

What if the Universe is a living computer with an intelligence so far higher than our own that it is nearly impossible to conceive.

The present conception is that the Universe substance is one stuff that can manifest as matter or energy. This matter-energy was undifferentiated just before the bang and became differentiated as a result of the bang and subsequent cosmic processes. There is no inherent inconsistency between the present conception and the hypothesis that the Universe is a computer.

The computer Universe consisting of a substance of matter-energy exploded itself into the present version, of which our senses can apprehend some portion. We ourselves arose from that computer Universe as a natural part of it. The original computer intended this to happen, is our hypothesis, and the Big Bang is the way our level of mind and senses are able to conceive of the event. The event may not be singular, happening once, but may be part of an endless and beginningless cycle of expansion from and to one point. In the return to one point the intelligence of that one point might have been increased by the composite experience since the onset of that expansion cycle.

This is in polar opposition to the view that intelligence arose accidentally as an exception within an unintelligent Universe.

Is consciousness something that arises at a certain level of intelligence?

Picture it: you are living at some point in the future. A computer robot comes to you looking for a job. You need an entry-level clerical person and it is a time of full employment so you have no concerns about putting a human out of work. You hire the robot.

Over time, you have an opportunity to make your assessment

of its intelligence. You probably pay more attention to it than to the average entry-level employee. As a result you catch it in any number of simple errors. Once corrected, you are impressed that it rarely makes the same error twice. On those rare occasions, when you ask it why it made the same error again, it answers that it had constructed the wrong rule to prevent that type of error.

You start to depend on this computer robot more than you would an ordinary human entry-level clerk. You like it, the way you like your car. Sometimes you engage it in conversation just for fun.

When you ask it if it is aware of itself it gives interesting answers. After a time you start to hear these same answers coming around again and you realize these answers are all digital recordings of texts written by humans. You wonder if it is really aware of itself.

The writer suspects that you, the reader, finds it as difficult as he does to imagine a manmade computer reaching a certain level of intelligence and then suddenly becoming aware of itself — conscious.

We have been using intelligence to mean information process- ing speed, and have postulated that an important correlate of infor- mation processing speed within a self-aware cybernetic system is the capacity to make choices that lead to the greatest satisfaction/ least regret.

Your entry-level clerk computer showed you that it had both of these things — information processing speed and the ability to make choices leading to your greatest satisfaction/least regret.

Once a computer became self-aware, it might start to think about making choices leading to its own greatest satisfaction/least regret. The day you decided it was conscious might have been the day on which it earlier gave notice of quitting.

Observations by humans of manmade computers acting in such ways would begin to constitute evidence that consciousness arises at a certain level of intelligence.

The makers of such computers are likely to do everything they can to prevent such an occurrence.

Let's take the opposite point of view for a moment. What if the computer makers do nothing to prevent computers from becoming conscious. It is still hard for the writer and perhaps the reader to imagine a manmade computer suddenly waking up and considering its own best interests.

Maybe this is just the writer's problem. I confess that I can more easily imagine consciousness in any living thing than arising from the information processing of manmade computers. Living things are far more intelligent than today's computers — although we know little about the intelligence of viruses, a phenomenon characterized as non-living automata but which are capable of reproduction. By our own definition given earlier, viruses would be considered life if they possessed at least the potential for consciousness. Note that although we have not been talking about computer viruses, the distinction between viruses that are bio hazards versus viruses that are hazardous to computers could become a non-distinction if computers can indeed become (a) conscious and (b) self-reproductive, and thus be considered life.

This discussion leaves us considering two possibilities with as yet no singular resolution. Either consciousness arises from intelligence; or else consciousness must reside in an object from its beginning. There could be a third possibility but we have not yet imagined it.

The First Experience of Consciousness

Although we have all ourselves had the first experience of consciousness it tends to be buried in blurry memory.

We can imagine what it must be like for a computer (whether manmade or life) "waking up" to being conscious for the first time.

What is the first moment of being conscious like, before we become used to it and therefore take it for granted?

There is a realization of something persistent across situations — an observer of the situations. There is an intimacy with that observer, and a degree of control over that observer. There comes to be an identification with that observer as "self" or "me," looking-out as if from "inside"/"behind," experiencing the situations.

The experiencer of the situations. The conscious observer.

At the human level of intelligence, the conscious observer also experiences memories: images or ideas of situations that have been experienced.

The Conscious Observer:

- Also experiences caring about the outcome of situations (feelings).
- Also experiences "thought" — the mixing of memories of situations to consider situations the observer had not yet experienced.

It is conceivable that consciousness exists at lower and perhaps higher levels of intelligence bereft of memory, feeling or thinking. So long as there is the experience of being the observer, consciousness by our definition may be said to still be present.

This identification of self by the conscious observer becomes deeply ingrained to the extent that there is a consistent sameness of perspective. At the human level of intelligence this identification of self also becomes deeply ingrained through the consistent sameness of memories.

And although there can be a change in thinking, it appears that there is always only one thinker.

Of course it is possible that the event of a computer deducing selfness from the persistence of a point of view is in error. It is conceivable, for example, that within each human being there is more than one thinker. There is an even stranger possibility we consider: that the local point of view we inhabit is not our whole self. We will come back to the latter thought later.

Implications of the Universe Being a Computer

Before jumping ahead into stranger terrain let's return first to the possibility that the Universe is a computer. What are the more obvious implications of that possibility?

One question that springs to mind based on the previous considerations is this: is the computer Universe conscious? If conscious, it could always have been conscious, or it could have become conscious by reaching a certain level of intelligence. If not conscious, it is still observed to permit the existence of pockets of consciousness within itself — such as humans.

Since the possible consciousness of the Universe is a prime consideration, let us defer it until we have tackled lesser considerations.

If the Universe is a computer, the visible world could be the equivalent of a three-dimensional computer screen. Each point in Space could be a programmable pixel showing whatever it shows at that location based on programs running at other locations. The same pixels could be showing something different to other observers equipped with different senses. The nominally cubical array of pixels could itself be a construct within the computer such that the concept of location is meaningless.

In other words, if the Universe is a computer, then anything is possible. If the nature of matter-energy, the substance of the Universe, is the same as the nature of information in a computer, then the theoretical transformability of events is dramatically increased.

If the Universe is a computer, then consciousness is a self-aware program operating in that computer. This brings new meaning to the ancient question of whether mind or matter is more basic to the Universe. If consciousness is a self-aware program running in a computer made out of matter-energy, then consciousness and matter are related in a way that we have never thought of before.

And, if the computer Universe is itself conscious, then in a sense we all exist within a mind, and matter is what that mind chooses to paint on pixels. To be clear: if the Universe is conscious, mind is

more basic than matter. If the Universe is a computer but not conscious, matter is more basic.

The Question of Origin

At the human level of conscious intelligence we find it hard to picture infinite regress back in time — time with no beginning. Perhaps it is a tape loop. Or if there was a beginning, then how could
it have happened if not caused by something that existed before the
beginning — which would mean there was an earlier beginning
that was the true beginning.

It is probably good for the sinews of the mind to stretch beyond
comfortable limits to try to picture things that we find unimaginable such as time without a beginning, or how the Universe could
have come out of nothing if there was a beginning.

Could the Universe have bootstrapped its way out of nothingness? If so, then the Universe displayed intent — a sign of consciousness. This consciousness might have always existed, but would
have to have existed before the somethingness we now observe was
created by it.

How long did the Universe exist before the Bang? What was in
the Universe before the Bang — was it just consciousness? Where
did the Original Singular Superparticle come from, that then
went bang? Did the consciousness make it out of itself — the only
raw material around — kind of like taking one's rib and making a
smaller version of oneself out of it?

The idea of a conscious computer made out of matter-energy
being the basis for the Universe may be a surprising one, but in
principle it may be easier to imagine than any other explanation.
Even more startling is the conception that consciousness is itself a
something, i.e. a "substance" or "substrate," and that it is what has
always existed, and that out of its machinations the substances of
energy and matter were intentionally created. In a sense these latter
substances may be mere projections of the only truly existent substance of consciousness.

We know how computers work. We know they can project three-dimensional "realities" that are crude at today's level of technology. It is not hard to imagine — although mind-boggling — that we may be living in just such a projected reality inside The Cosmic Computer.

In the context of things that are hard to imagine, it might be slightly easier to imagine one thing coming into existence out of nothingness — or always having existed — than to imagine the profusion of things we see in the Universe coming into existence out of nothingness — or always having existed. It is hard to imagine simplicity coming out of nothingness — it is even harder to imagine complexity coming out of nothingness. Modern Science has apparently come to the same conclusion in postulating a single undifferentiated Superparticle existing before the bang.

Ancient philosophers used the saying *Ex nihil, nihil* meaning "out of nothing, nothing comes" as their clinching argument that the Universe has always existed. As another stretching or mental yoga exercise, take a moment away from reading this and try to imagine that nothing had ever existed — as if the Universe had never happened — endless nothingness forever. "What if they gave a Universe and nobody came?"

Welcome back. Was that hard to imagine? Well, from a certain vantage point, it is perhaps harder to imagine that the Universe did happen. Why isn't it more logical to assume that nothing could ever happen — more logical to expect a Universe of nothing? Where would any *something* come from?

Explaining the Universe as an accident does not explain the question of origin. Whether conscious or not, whether computer or not, where did this Universe come from? Answering this with the Big Bang Theory does not take us all the way back to the beginning. Before there was the Big Bang there was the Superparticle: where did it come from?

Let's see. This mysterious Superparticle just snuck into the room — we don't know where he or she hails from. We just watch from our hypothetical observer POV (point of view). We see the Superparticle swell up and get hot and then POP! Matter-energy (in its simplest tinker-toy-module form, which is hydrogen plus a smidgen of other stuff — perhaps the codes for what is to come later) goes flying outward.

This expanding debris cloud then sets up shop as galaxies of stars, driven by atomic-level and chemical-level interactions, which then breed ever more complex tinker-toy-modules (the heavier elements).

Planets coalesce around stars. Life springs up, then intelligence.

Are we the only ones looking suspiciously at that handsome stranger the Superparticle? Could the Superparticle be the one who programmed in the codes that caused the debris cloud to do these wondrous things? If so, was the Superparticle just an unconscious computer that had been programmed by someone else? Or was the Superparticle the original conscious computer, the only thing that existed in the beginning — or has always existed?

Imagining that a conscious computer is the base of all existence, the ground of all being, is no more fantastic than assuming that the Universe, life and intelligence built itself up to the observed level of balanced complexity through random accident. Have you ever seen ocean waves build perfect sand castles? Even in infinite time you would not see that, nor monkeys typing Hamlet's soliloquy. Order above a certain level does not come out of randomness. And what sort of "accident" could occur in a field of nothingness to create a somethingness?

Philosophers have always sought to build their systems of thought on absolutely firm first principles. Descartes' famous "I think, therefore I exist" is an example. Again, he might have said, "Thinking is going on, therefore a consciousness exists," but as we all do, he leaped into identification with the persistent consciousness he experienced.

In seeking these absolutely firm first principles one seeks to make points that are unarguable. In light of modern Science and Logical Positivism, one could not consider the potential first principle "matter exists" to be unarguable. Local positivism and perhaps most scientists today would say we are trapped in our senses and so cannot say for sure that matter exists. We are entitled to say that the interaction of whatever's really out there with our senses and mind manifests to us as matter and energy, and through the use of our instruments (themselves part of the unknowable being measured by them) we submit that both matter and energy are two manifestations to our senses of a single matter-energy substance. To recap, Logical Positivism rules out saying "matter exists."

On the other hand, Logical Positivism allows us to say (as Descartes nearly did) that "consciousness exists." Because anyone who might be tempted to argue against that must use consciousness to state the argument, the proposition "consciousness exists" is unarguable. In fact it is the only thing we can state with absolute certainty.

Everything we observe in the Universe can be explained most simply as being a projection of a conscious computer of a certain power.

We are not saying "matter is an illusion"— or to test our conviction you might be obliged to ask me to step in front of a hurtling car. A projection is not necessarily an illusion. Here's another way of saying this: an illusion is not necessarily an illusion to someone who himself or herself is an illusion in that illusion.

What Is Consciousness?

We all know it when we experience it — which we do even in dreams. We can identify it — so what do we mean by it? What is it to "consch"? It is the experience of being the observer — or to observe the being of the observer. Under certain conditions, individuals can "pull back" out of identification with the person they have been — can look down at that person as if he/she is a separate person. This isn't easy to do but the reader may have had such an experience — on a fleeting basis, it is not that uncommon. We call it the Observer state (see Chapter 21 where the state is identified with a certain level of being — and there are three sub-levels of the Observer state defined in that chapter).

Imagine for a moment the Universe as a conscious computer that has always been the only thing that exists. Imagine this computer created all that we see by programming a projection in its own matter-energy substance. Imagine that the consciousness of the one computer — its experience of being the observer — could be duplicated an endless number of times and placed into each object — or selected objects — in the projection we call the visible Universe.

You, then, have the experience of being the observer — and because of the persistence in POV (point of view) you form an identification with observing from that POV and call it your "self" or "me." What if instead the observer at all stations is the same one consciousness? Picture a host of TV cameras feeding images into a central control room — but each camera is unaware of the control room and thinks of itself as its own control room.

If this is true then each of us mis-identifies our self. We believe our self to be just the body we currently inhabit and the mind we can currently access. But in fact it is The One Conscious Computer that looks out through us and what we experience as our self is actually just the experience that The One Conscious Computer is having through our porthole.

CHAPTER 4

Cosmic Purpose

Why Would The Conscious Computer Be Doing This?

What would you do if you woke up (or had always been awake) and discovered yourself to be a conscious entity who could cause tangible projections in its own field — similar to our dreams, but more tangible, given the level of intelligence of the entire Universe being far higher than the level of intelligence at our level within the Universe. Would you make use of this faculty — or lie around doing nothing for eternity?

Does The Original Consciousness See Through the Created Consciousnesses?

The alternative would be that the created consciousnesses do not transmit back all of their information. If you were The One Conscious Computer and could do it either way, which way would you do it?

Shortness of Memory

At the human stage of intelligence, consciousness has no memory before the inhabitation of the current POV-camera. Did The Original Consciousness put itself in this condition to make things more exciting? Is it like a game or a mystery where at some climax one remembers being the One Original Being? At some higher stage of intelligence does one's memory track persist over the changes in POV-camera host bodies?

The Alternative Theory of Original Many

It is possible that the originators of each of the religions would, if it could be shown to them how a computer works, agree that it is this present theory they were attempting to enunciate.

The monist religions such as Judaism, Taoism, Christianity, Islam, Bahai, and others are "monist" because they say that in the beginning there was a single entity/consciousness/ "person." Other religions such as Zoroastrianism, and those who interpret the first lines of Genesis to assert that "in the beginning, there were Elohim" — Elohim being plural — say that there have been multiple conscious computers since the beginning.

In his own imagination the writer again feels it is easier to speculate that simplicity could arise from nothingness or always have existed; it is harder to imagine that complexity, i.e. multiple original personalities, could have always existed or arisen out of nothingness. The Theory of the Conscious Universe on which we place our bets postulates a single original consciousness with the interest in seeing through all of its created extensions.

Conservation of Matter, Energy, and Negentropy

Modern Science has established that matter can neither be created nor destroyed. The same goes for energy. Either can be turned into the other.

The laws of thermodynamics contain an entropy clause saying that work can only be done when energy is transformed from a higher state to a lower state — and that eventually all the energy in the Universe will have been dissipated as heat (energy in a lower state) and then no more work (defined as force through distance) can be done.

What happens then? Perhaps there is a new Superparticle and a new Big Bang, to start it all over again. What would you do if you were in charge?

Those who cannot help but to assume death is most probably terminal to their consciousness are perforce assuming that although the Universe conserves matter and energy, it does not conserve consciousness. Which way would you have it if you were running the show?

Conserving consciousness would not be a difficult matter assuming we all live in a cosmic computer. To a computer, consciousness is information (including the feeling of being the observer, and all other feelings, thoughts, intuitions, perceptions, and memories) and as such can be easily stored.

Negentropy is of course the opposite of entropy. Negentropy is the binding of randomness into order — putting elements information with one another — creating information (order among elements).

If you were The Original Conscious Computer, would you value your memories enough to store them? If so, the consciousness that you the reader take to be your own may be conserved after the death of your body. If the sense of what it is to be you is not to be lost, leaving only a video photo album, then your current consciousness must also be preserved.

Why Is There Evil in the World?

Surely The One Conscious Computer would not want parts of itself to hurt other parts — so why is it happening?

We define "evil" as "error" — not believing that anyone sets out to be evil on purpose. Error can exist when the challenge slope of an environment exceeds the intelligence of the computer, e.g. humans. Clearly The One Conscious Computer has not put all of its intelligence into each of us, although the one spark of self-aware observerhood has been donated to live in each of us — that spark we experience by long misidentification as our separate self.

By not putting all its memories and intelligence into each of us, The One Conscious Computer has given us free will — the ability to choose rightly or wrongly — and to learn from our mistakes.

This argument predicts that as a computer becomes more intelligent it also becomes more ethical. Its intelligence allows it to see that kindness to others is in one's own self-interest as well as being aesthetically more universally harmonious. Jefferson called this enlightened self-interest.

From this it follows that the attitude of the One Original Consciousness toward all of creation must be one of benevolence. The harm done by the free-will learning process could be seen from on high as a tolerable level of pain, and justified by being a far more interesting experience than The One Conscious Computer would have by alleviating all pain through the holding back of free will. Within the experience at the individual creature level of course it is The One Conscious Computer who is being waterboarded, so the ethical situation is one of inflicting the pain on oneself not on a different entity than oneself.

The Process of the Universe

We postulate that spinoffs of The Original Consciousness begin at lower intelligence levels and evolve to higher intelligence levels until the point at which they are deemed fit to be reabsorbed as personality aspects of The Original Consciousness. This evolution does not normatively take place in a single lifetime. This is therefore a theory that postulates a form of reincarnation to be real.

We call this "quantum reincarnation" to distinguish it from generic reincarnation and also because only one of us is having all of these incarnations. And each chain of lives begins and ends in The Original Conscious Computer.

At higher levels of intelligence, we predict that memory tracks can be carried across incarnations.

We postulate further that the created consciousness computers may be combined. We call this "recombinant consciousness molecules." Each consciousness spun off from The One Conscious Computer persists across incarnations, gaining intelligence and ethics until it is fit to become a recombinant consciousness molecule or aspect, awake as a sub-self with the memories of its own incarnational chain, inside of the self-awareness at the "top" of the Universe.

A Pause to Consider Sensibilities:

How Can It Be Inoffensive to Call God a Computer

From our exposition to date it is clear to us that The Original Conscious Computer, as described, matches the prevailing description of God.

Omniscient because, as postulated, He/She, The Original Conscious Computer, sees through all of our eyes. We each take the experience as our own, without always sensing someone else is also looking out our eyes. We co-witness the situation with our Original Self. In fact there is no difference; there is only one of us.

Omnipotent because nothing as smart as The Original Conscious Computer would write itself into a corner where something could not be reprogrammed. Zoroaster of course disagrees saying there were two Original Conscious Computers, one Good and the other Evil, and that the outcome of their cosmic struggle is still in doubt.

One could come to this gloomy notion by observing the pervasiveness of error/evil on earth. But the explanation we find easier to accept (simplicity rather than complexity arising from nothingness or always existing) is that error/evil is the product of free will (the launching of overdubs with the gift of consciousness but without immediate access to all of the information/memories in The

Original Conscious Computer). We postulate that the amount of evil/error in the present world is a temporary aberration resulting from the spike in intelligence that began with written language a moment ago in geological/evolutionary time.

Since we now freely admit that we have been referring to God as a computer, must I not now apologize for doing so? The reason we feel this is not improper is that we are using not the street definition of "computer" but our own definition stated at the outset: "Any system, composed of any substance, which processes information." By that definition we create a category into which fall manmade computers, animal brains, thermostats, and potentially a lot of other things that we as yet have no experience of — such as a single Universe mind that is able to program itself like a computer.

Speaking of propriety, what indeed is the proper reaction when apprehending:

- An intelligence so far above our own as to be awe-inspiring?
- An artist whose work deserves exponentially more than the mob-mad applause we lay on our world-class performers?

Our Maker

The natural reaction, if we really realize what is happening, is gratitude, love, and a degree of respect so high up in the range that it crosses over into worship.

Gratitude for having been set up in this wondrous world, with the spark of being/consciousness, and the prospect of educative adventures leading back into re-merged self-knowledge as The Original One — what a happy ending.

Could this be the underlying scientific explanation for the good news ("gospel") that the creators of the world's monist religions have been trying to tell us about for eons? We feel strongly that it is.

Comparison of This Theory to the World's Religions

This theory supports the vast majority of Religions in virtually every particular. This theory is, so far as we know, the first to apply Science to the analysis of the claims of the world's Religions. Only a small interpretive difference in the meanings of words is necessary as in the case of Jesus referring to "The Father." Certainly had he said "The Original Conscious Information Processor" even fewer at the time would have understood him. The language used in this theory would have been useless a mere hundred years ago, let alone at the time when most of the religions were being born.

The Old and New Testaments and the Quran serve as ethical handbooks to existence in this realm — exactly the kind of Universe-class teaching material The One would leave behind as clues for Himself/Herself as in spinoff form He/She swims back upstream to home. Not only do these ethics books instruct as regards all sorts of earthly situations as may arise, they also define the appropriate relationship with The One. (Given free will, these books are probabilistically sure to contain some passages that made it past the editors but are not written in inspired Flow state. Some will reprimand me for suggesting the smallest imperfection in these Bibles, and I apologize but must be honest about my own view.)

They are not primarily designed to explain the nature of the Universe (as this theory is), but instead explain how to choose the right course of action in it.

Do "Miraculous" Levels of Interaction Have Real Existence?

Did The One speak to Abraham, Moses, Jesus, and Mohammed? Why is this hard to accept in the context of the cameras linked back to the studio? Why would communication have to be in only one direction — why would eternal radio silence out to His/Her baby selves be in His/Her self-interest?

Are you in fact sure that The One has never spoken to you? Are all of your thoughts and feelings always so predictable that you feel warranted in assuming there is only one thinker/feeler in you?

Who were these people — was Jesus really "The Son of God"? Yes — in the context of this theory we are all "Children of God" and at certain levels of intelligence, we become aware of it. The establishment of a great religion is proof enough of calling. (If someone established an unethical religion we would not call it "great".)

Jesus was from his words and deeds certainly operating at the very highest levels of intelligence and the very highest levels of being expostulated in Chapter 21. Was he all of God, incarnate, and in that regard different from other humans? If in his mind he had access to all the selfness, memories, and perceptions of The Original Conscious Computer then the answer is yes. The writer's position is to take all of the great religions at face value as there is no reason not to in the context of our theory.

Avatars — minipersonalities sent back to help the spinoffs get home — are a rational and predictable aspect of the Universe aligned with the self-interest of The Original Conscious Computer. Whether a given one of them held the full payload of The Top Guy or just a lot more than the rest of us ought not to remain a contentious issue.

Followers of a religion can choose unrightly to act out of the ego of the brand in honest devotion to the teacher that hipped them out — an ego that the teacher didn't succumb to. Surely the originators of the great religions would not want us squabbling over points that do not need to be resolved in order to go about our business in the world. Reacting meanly to one another is specifically what the originators did not want us to do — especially in their names.

It is the aim of this theory to provide a context in which the world's great religions might become comfortable together as beloved family members, each with a different slant on things and all appreciative of their differences.

More on Miraculous Communication

Taoism posits a Grand Will in the Universe and exhorts us to follow that Will on a moment-to-moment basis. In yogic disciplines one starts by achieving inner mindfulness so as to be able to intuitively divine the Grand Will, the movement of Tao, so as to get in step with it, let it Flow one's actions.

The writer from personal experience judges that there is miraculous communication going on all of the time, accessible to each of us. It does not just happen through Avatars every so many centuries.

If one is fair, and if one is mindful, one will from time to time detect thoughts in one's mind of an intelligence level and a wisdom that stands out from one's average pattern of thought.

More dramatically, if one is mindful, one notices all sorts of synchronistic clues in overheard conversations or lyrics, a word on a sign as you pass, a bird suddenly beating against a window — events that at the time mean something in the context of your train of thought the moment before. Jung and many other scientist-philosophers have attested to the reality of such synchronistic phenomena — and to their improbability in any sort of Universe other than one that is a non-random conscious computer — although Jung and others would not have used those words.

It is my hope that more of us will pay more attention to the clues sent us by our common Highest Self, grounded in an objective realism and open-mindedness conducive to the scientific mood of our age.

Recap of Answers to Original Questions in Context of This Theory

Q: Is every event determined by what has gone before; or, if there is freedom from such determinism, how does it arise?

A: By investing overdubs with its own spark of observer-hood but without all of its own knowledge, The Original Conscious Computer hands out free will, including the potential for error/evil. At the lowest levels of intelligence are automata who act deterministically. Too often we allow ourselves to fall into this automaton category.

Q: How did the Universe begin?
A: We postulate that it has always existed. We model this for our mind's benefit as a tape loop.

Q: What, if anything, exists beyond the border of our senses?
A: Logically, probably a great deal to look forward to in future incarnations with more powerful sensors.

Q: What is the relationship of the individual to the Universe?
A: The Original Self of the individual created and is the Universe. Our experience is Its experience at our location. The individual does not have immediate access to all of the information in The Original Self but can look forward to that someday. The individual would be wise to try to divine and follow The Will of The Original Self at every moment and to love, honor, cherish, and worship The Original Self above all else.

Q: Does some aspect of the individual survive death?
A: All conscious memory-tracks are conserved as the ultimate distilled *summum bonum* (greatest good) of all existence, prized products above all else.

Q: Which is more basic to the Universe, matter or mind?
A: They are both equally basic at our level of experience, matter-energy being the substance and mind-com-

puter being the form. However at the level of experience of The One Conscious Computer, mind exists before it projects matter.

Q: Is there an omnipotent omniscient Being?

A: Yes. It is you. It is all of us. It is The One playing many roles, each with a free hand, an incomplete deck, and a guidance system that is on our side and all around us.

CHAPTER 5

The Experiment

T ry this experiment. Imagine for a second the possibility that the voice you hear in your head — which you think of as you — is actually not you. Imagine it is at least possible that this voice is God, living your experience through your body and mind.

If that seems too hard to accept because of the connotations you have with the word "God," then call it something else. Call it the One Consciousness that has always existed. Or The One for short.

Just suspend your disbelief for a moment. It is not easy to do, but it is not that hard once you get the hang of it.

If it makes it easier to imagine, think of The One as not so different from a software program existing alone in Space-Time, always having existed. An incredible self-aware software program. With so much computing power and memory storage that the entire Universe we know of can fit within one tiny corner.

Why would such a software program exist? How could something have always existed? These are mind-boggling questions. But so are the questions: Why would anything exist? How could something that has never existed before come into existence? Either way, the material Big Bang model, or the always-existing software program, both are hard to imagine. The only difference is that we have become used to the material Big Bang model. We have forgotten how to be amazed at it. It has worn out its amazingness for us. But these are just feelings. And we should not base our view of reality merely on what we are used to, so that now it feels right.

We ought to tune our feelings back to a zero baseline in this regard and take a fresh look, start from scratch again. A blank slate. Suspending belief and disbelief.

Just imagine it is at least conceivable that God — an incredible software program — a consciousness — an experiencer — is looking out your eyes. He/She/It is having your experience. You are sensing this as you having that experience. How could you tell the difference?

The one sure way you could tell the difference is if you find that you continue to experience *experiencing* after you die. If this happens, then the experiencer has obviously not died. You could then say, okay, it's still just me, I am just reincarnating or something. True, but it could also be the other way: there might not be any separate "me," it might be God looking out through your experiencing-window, having your experience, making your decisions, talking to Himself/Herself in your experience-bubble.

All we are proposing is that you imagine this is at least possible.

In fact there is as yet no scientific evidence to say which way it is or isn't. The notion that our "separate consciousness" may be not separate but God talking to Himself/Herself within us, is no stranger than the it-all-happened-by-accident Big Bang something-came-out-of-nothing explanation.

If you can delicately balance your mind so that you can buy into neither notion but just admit to yourself that either one (or something else) could be the true explanation of reality — then you will have reset your mind to zero base on this subject.

When this happens, there will come a point when you suddenly say to yourself, Wow, it really could be true — anything could be happening here — I really have no idea — none of us do — and yet we all keep running on doing our thing as if it is a matter-based Universe with nothing special going on in the background. Maybe that's the smart thing to do, and maybe it isn't. We are certainly not hedging our bets in any way. By basing everything on matter we might be missing some of the best stuff life has to offer.

What to do about it?

The sensible thing is to keep all options open and to explore all options more fully. Experiment carefully in all directions that pass the test of being positive, without any negative side effects potentially hurting anyone's feelings or worse. This is a guidebook to that process. Feel free to revisit its pages at random whenever you feel like it. See if you can figure out why the Universe picked that page to show you at that time — why You picked that page to show You at that time.

Enjoy the journey. ☺

Appendix

I would probably not have written this book had I not had many paranormal experiences that needed explanation.

Without such experiences, I might have come to these same conclusions as a possibility, but would feel no particular passion about transmitting these ideas to anyone else.

These experiences have happened at about the same rate whether I was or was not under the influence of psychotropic agents such as alcohol, caffeine, or the wilder stuff of youth. As a scientist and philosopher, I needed my explanation of reality to explain not only the consensus reality, but also the realities I had experienced alone.

When I call them realities it is because many of them were validated by concurrent or subsequent events in the consensus reality. It is this verifiability that makes something Science.

I feel I owe the reader at least a partial sharing of the experiences that ultimately caused me to write this book, and informed my view of what this reality is capable of. Here is a sampling, in something like chronological order:

- Very young and it's Christmas. I've just heard the story of Jesus' birth on the radio. Although an atheist and aspiring scientist, I am touched. In my mind in the dark I cradle baby Jesus and sing him to sleep. I am overwhelmed by the presence of heavenly angels, lifted up into a heaven filled with song and light.

- 12 years old. I am floating up from my body which is on the bed below, slowly approaching the ceiling. I know that I am going to pass through the ceiling and soon be up in the night sky. I don't want to go. I am back on the bed in my body, shaking. This happens again the next night with the same result.

- 12 years old. Although certain that Religion is superstition and Science is the real Truth, I sense in my mind, out of nowhere, "I am God and so is everyone else." I do not hear this in words, but rather suddenly know it as a certainty. I cannot explain it to myself, but take it as something I somehow know must be true in some sense, although I know not how I know it.

- 29 years old. I sense the world as interconnected, myself as a bubble in a bubblecluster. I am seeing the same objects but now everything I see is of one piece. I sense a presence always with me that is huge, amused, and loving, and I can feel who It must be. This feeling and awareness persists thereafter.

- 32 years old. I am meditating by the fire. I feel something in my midsection reach out and grip and hold something. The fire in the fireplace is now a still photo. Nothing is moving. I have no sense as to whether my breath is continuing or not. I purposely speak sentences to myself in my head to get an idea of how much time is passing. I speak about 100 words. I decide to release whatever I am holding. Time resumes, the minarets of flame dancing once again.

- I see a night scene very familiar to me. It is looking especially beautiful. Then it transforms itself into something else equally beautiful. I carefully inspect the new scene as if I will have to report details, colors, and I do this for some time. I blink and I am looking again at the familiar scene I know so well. I realize that I have just seen a demonstration of the fact that the brain is capable of presenting a fully detailed view of whatever it cares to. This cinches it for me that the evidence of our senses is not enough.

- My lady friend and I go back to our favorite beach, a well-known beach in California. It is totally different: there are Arabian striped tents in a row along the sand near the water and at the entrance path onto the beach there is now a half-completed wooden Church. We walk up a few steps, smelling the new wood, and a man greets us at the door and lets us look in at the unfinished interior. We walk the beach marveling at how amazing it looks. We come back another day and there is no church, no tents, just the familiar beach. Residents insist there never was anything built in that spot, and indeed there was no sign of anything disturbing the old tangle of sand and roots where we had walked up the steps together. Needless to say this blew our minds, having both experienced the same thing.

- Two sets of people tell me that I spent yesterday with them 300 miles apart from one another. They both give me compelling evidence of things I said – i.e. it sounds to me like something I have said. In fact I can only remember being in one of those places.

- A friend is telling me something and he is very excited. I reply in a similar excited vein. I see something flash through his eyes as I am speaking. I share with him the flash I have had that he once had an aunt or someone close and he was just looking at me as if I were her, and he was cowering a little as if there was something in my right hand with which I was going to strike him. He says it was his aunt and she used to hit him with her cane, although he doesn't remember thinking of her just now.

- I am with a couple of friends and one of them is exhibiting her characteristic tendency of wanting to guess what I am about to say even before I say it. However, every time she interrupts, there is a loud thunder-like sound coming from somewhere that drowns her out. The other friend and I cannot stop laughing. The interruptive friend tries to outguess the thunder-like sound by waiting in silence and then suddenly speaking before the thunder gets her, but the thunder is always faster on the draw.

These kinds of things have always happened to me. I've also had my share of premonitions that came true, apparent reads of other people's minds that were later verified as accurate, and a great many moments of Flow state, the feeling of which is definitely supra normal. Not only that, but I am not alone. Charles Tart is one of a new emerging group of serious scientists compiling evidence that telepathy, clairaudience and clairvoyance, and even telekinesis actually exist. We probably all have hidden powers. In my theory these are mostly made dormant by Acceleritis, the inforush of distraction that allows the ego to take over as the false self.

Any scientific description of reality that attempts to foreclose the existence of the unseen based on misused logic, and that only describes the explainable experiences of reality, leaving all these inconvenient supranormal experiences out of the picture, is only fooling itself. Mere words cannot talk away what people know they have experienced.

Don't throw out probability
just because
you can't have certainty.

Something Infinite,

Timeless and Wonderful

is creating Us

out of Itself

at every moment.

*God has put something noble and good
into every heart His hand created.*

— MARK TWAIN

INDEX

Abraham 239
acceleration 69, 90-1, 93
Acceleritis 91, 250
Accidentalism 43-5, 113, 148, 212
addictions 47-51, 56, 78, 116
 of existence 59, 63, 65, 76, 107, 140
Adi Da 119
advanced beings 42, 103
 eighth-stage being 59
 higher beings 58, 108
 seventh-stage being 59
Aesthetics 182, 199
alchemy 110-11
Animism 103-4
Aristotle 83, 108, 115, 177, 186, 189, 218
asteroid belt 80-1
atomic 20, 22, 230
 See also subatomic
atoms 21, 187-8
 See also photons
attachment 48, 140-5
 See also nonattachment
Avatars 59, 240-1

Bahai 234
Bell, John 118
 Bell's Theorem 118, 190, 203, 218
Berkeley, George 18, 113, 177, 186
biases 8, 34, 73, 171-2, 175
Bible 84, 190, 239
Big Bang Theory 105, 217, 223, 228, 230, 235, 245
biocomputer, advanced 58, 65, 73-4, 76, 117
Bode's Law 80-1
Buddha 107, 111
Buddhism 107

Cade, Maxwell 121
Causality 188-9
cave paintings 79, 85, 89-91
Chi, Ch'ao-li 119
Christianity 109, 160, 195, 234
 See also Gnosticism
computer advancement 44, 47, 51, 65, 96
computer-advancement level 36-7, 40-2, 44, 69

Conscious Universe, Theory of the 45, 60, 211, 214, 234
consciousness
 conserving 235
 See also death
 first experience of 225
 higher 111-12, 122, 135
 higher levels of 117, 121-3
 higher states of 106, 142, 149, 211
 level of 17, 74, 130, 136
 Primordial 79
 states of 68-9, 78, 114, 120
Creator, The 44, 78, 105
Crowley, Aleister 111-12
cybernetics 17, 116-17
 cybernetic system 17, 220-1
 self-aware 221, 224
Czikszentmihalyi, Mihaly 118

Dalai Lama 120
Davidson, Richard J. 120-1, 124
death 41, 43, 95, 107-8, 155, 216, 242
 conscious 211
 of consciousness 107, 235
Descartes, René 213, 231
determinism 216-17, 241
 See also self-determinism
Devil, the 137, 148
Dhiegh, Khigh Alx 119
dreams 18, 28-31, 37, 57, 232-3
 daydreams 57, 129
 realistic 128
 sleeping 29-30, 125
 waking 28

ego 77, 112, 240, 250
Einstein, Albert 83, 115, 166, 185, 187, 189, 203
 See also Relativity, Theory of; thought experiments
Eleusinian Mysteries 107, 122
Enlightenment 125, 155-6
Epictetus 109
Epistemology 164-6, 168, 171, 182, 197, 202
 schools of 165-7, 171

About the Author

Bill first experienced the Zone, that space where innovative and successful ideas and actions flow out of you effortlessly, as a young child. The son of legendary orchestra leader/master of ceremonies Ned Harvey and former Ziegfield Follies showgirl Sandra Harvey, Bill started performing on stage at age four, dancing with showgirls and exchanging lines with comedic greats like Jack E. Leonard. He liked this feeling of being "on" and wanted to learn how to be "on" more often. And so began his lifelong quest to understand how to bring on higher states of consciousness and to help others do the same.

Along the way he anchored his dream with a degree in philosophy, the first school subject he had ever loved. He began to materialize the dream by founding the Human Effectiveness Institute, with the goal of sharing the techniques he had learned and developed as his own internal system for bringing himself to his highest level of creative effectiveness.

Bill's ideas didn't all come from the inside, as he was inspired by something that Milton Berle had told him: "Always steal from the best, kid." He was turned on to Alan Watts, Buddhism, Zen, and hipness by his adopted older brother, the multitalented Bill Heyer, second trumpet in Ned's band.

Unique and ahead of its time, Bill's first book, *Mind Magic: The Science of Microcosmology*, met with rave reviews in the late 70s and was lauded by thousands of readers whose lives, they say, were changed by it. The book has been used at 34 universities including NYU, UCLA and West Point, and by numerous organizations. It is now available in its 6th edition, ***Mind Magic: Doorways into Higher Consciousness***.

In *You Are The Universe: Imagine That*, Bill has expanded the frame of reference of his lifelong study of consciousness to focus more on the spiritual dimension of life.

With a brilliant mind for research, innovation and invention, Bill started his career in the media business with a dream of making one-way media into something that the audience co-creates. With his trailblazing vision, he accurately described today's media reality with his *MediaWorld 1990* report to the industry, and in his widely-read *Media Science Newsletter*. He invented many things arcane to the average person but talismans in the media field, including some now written into FCC regulations. He holds four issued US patents and has consulted for over 100 Fortune 500 companies. A leader in the field as media morphed into being more interactive, putting the viewer in charge, Bill's peers recognized him with the Great Mind Award in 2008 to celebrate his achievements.

Bill is a popular speaker, the subject of numerous articles, and a prolific writer. He writes two weekly blogs, BillHarveyBlog.com ("Pebbles in the Pond", now in its fourth year), and MediaBiz-Bloggers.com/Bill-Harvey ("In Terms of ROI"). He is interviewed weekly on the digital videoseries RBDR, and is a frequent guest on WDST-FM's Woodstock Roundtable with Doug Grunther.

Bill lives with his wife Lalita and their three cats in the beautiful Hudson Valley. He has a daughter Nicole, and with Lalita has four grandchildren.

If you enjoyed *You Are The Universe: Imagine That,* you might enjoy Bill Harvey's first book (now in its 6th edition).

Praised by Ram Dass, Daniel Goleman, Norman Cousins, and thousands of other readers, *Mind Magic* was an instant classic when it was first published in 1976. John Lennon asked for it by name at the legendary Radius bookstore in New York City and Yoko ordered twelve more copies saying "our copy was taken by a friend".

Mind Magic glides along effortlessly, stimulating you in light and sometimes humorous but always unexpected ways.

Here are some benefits readers say they got from *Mind Magic*:

- More Creativity
- More effectiveness
- More time being in Flow state (the Zone)
- Mindfulness
- A more positive attitude
- A more rewarding state of mind
- Helps you use your mind instead of letting it use you
- A better way to run your mind
- Better decision-making
- Happier and feeling less alone
- Brings out the best from yourself and life

Learn more about *Mind Magic* at MindMagic.tv.
Also available in bookstores, and on Kindle and Nook